CONTENTS   HISTORY OF SPEED

ACKNOWLEDGEMENTS

The one-line mentions on this page do not do justice to the skill and work that goes into producing a volume such as this, from initial idea through to the finished product you see in front of you.

I've collaborated with designer Craig Lamb and production editor Pauline Hawkins on a number of projects, and once again they've been a pleasure to work with. As ever, I am indebted to them for their efforts and patience.

Mortons' wider publishing team must also be afforded great credit – Holly Furness for the superb cover adorning this edition and picture desk operators Paul Fincham and Jonathan Schofield for ensuring the imagery featured is of the high quality required.

Speaking of imagery, Jon Day at the Motoring Picture Library has been most helpful in making the necessary searches of the rich archive he manages. Without the wonderful photography and his efforts, it would have been difficult to get this bookazine off the ground.

And as ever I have enjoyed fantastic personal support throughout, making it possible to spend the time researching and writing about this wonderful subject.

design_lamb@btinternet.com

COVER DESIGN:
Holly Furness

PRODUCTION EDITOR:
Pauline Hawkins

REPROGRAPHICS:
Paul Fincham
Jonathan Schofield

ADVERTISING:
Billy Manning
bmanning@mortons.co.uk

MARKETING MANAGER:
Charlotte Park

COMMERCIAL DIRECTOR:
Nigel Hole

PUBLISHING DIRECTOR:
Dan Savage

PUBLISHER:
Steve O'Hara

❖ Images marked ○ are in the public domain
❖ Images marked ✱ are published under a Creative Commons Licence, creativecommons.org
❖ Images credited Press Association are courtesy of PA Images
❖ Images credited MPL are courtesy of the Motoring Picture Library
❖ Images credited SSC are courtesy of SSC Programme Ltd

PRINTED BY:
William Gibbons and Sons, Wolverhampton

ISBN:
978-1-911276-42-5

PUBLISHED BY:
Mortons Media Group Ltd
Media Centre
Morton Way
Horncastle
Lincolnshire
LN9 6JR

COPYRIGHT:
Mortons Media Group Ltd
2017 all rights reserved.

Year	Speed
1898	39.24
1898	41.42
1899	43.69
1899	49.92
1899	57.60
1899	65.79
1902	75.06
1902	76.08
1902	76.60
1902	77.13
1903	83.47
1903	84.73
1904	94.78
1904	97.25
1904	103.56
1904	104.52
1905	109.65
1906	121.57
1909	125.95
1914	124.12
1922	133.75
1924	143.31
1924	146.01
1925	146.16
1925	150.76
1926	152.33
1926	169.30
1926	171.02
1927	174.88
1927	203.79
1928	206.96
1928	207.55
1929	231.45
1931	246.09
1932	253.97
1933	272.46
1935	276.82
1935	301.13
1937	312.00
1938	345.50
1938	350.20
1938	357.50
1939	369.70
1947	394.20
1963	407.45
1964	403.10
1964	413.20
1964	434.02
1964	468.72
1964	526.28
1964	536.71
1965	555.48
1965	576.55
1965	600.60
1970	630.39
1983	633.47
1997	714.14
1997	763.07
????	1000MPH?

THE EVOLUTION OF SPEED

This story begins with a rather serene run of 39.24mph in the French countryside, and culminates with a supersonic roar of 763.07mph across a desert in Nevada. At the very basic level, both events were man and machine pushing past what people believed to be possible and finding a level beyond. But the incredible difference in the speeds achieved demonstrates just how far the land speed record has progressed in the 120 years since its inception.

Without any doubt, advancements in technology and engineering have been pivotal. The development of the petrol engine, a greater understanding of aerodynamics, the embracing of jet power, the deployment of rocket propulsion… all have had a crucial impact. Whatever the tools available though, the key driver behind the mind-boggling increases is sheer human ingenuity and desire.

From 1898 through to 1997 and beyond, this potent combination has fuelled a relentless pursuit of speed – and it's spawned a truly remarkable competition that has produced some fascinating characters and their weird and wonderful machines.

It has been my absolute pleasure to tell their tales in the 132 pages before you; I sincerely hope I've done it the justice it so clearly deserves.

Jack Harrison
Author

RECORDS HOLDERS BY NATION

10 GREAT BRITAIN

8 FRANCE

7 USA

3 BELGIUM

1 IRELAND

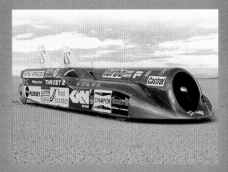

Gaston de Chasseloup-Laubat
The first fastest man

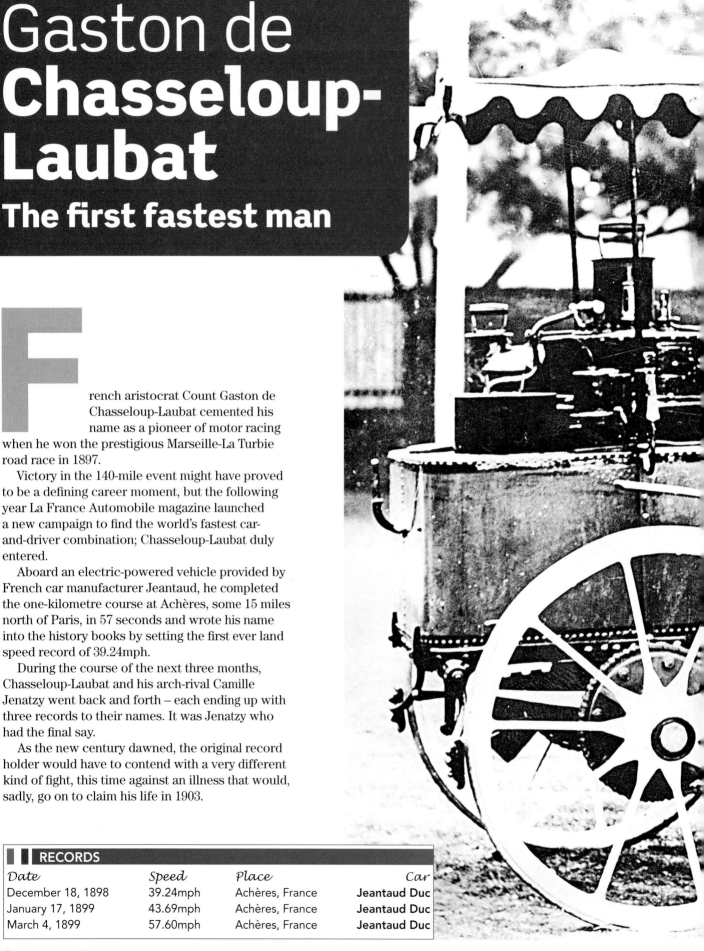

French aristocrat Count Gaston de Chasseloup-Laubat cemented his name as a pioneer of motor racing when he won the prestigious Marseille-La Turbie road race in 1897.

Victory in the 140-mile event might have proved to be a defining career moment, but the following year La France Automobile magazine launched a new campaign to find the world's fastest car-and-driver combination; Chasseloup-Laubat duly entered.

Aboard an electric-powered vehicle provided by French car manufacturer Jeantaud, he completed the one-kilometre course at Achères, some 15 miles north of Paris, in 57 seconds and wrote his name into the history books by setting the first ever land speed record of 39.24mph.

During the course of the next three months, Chasseloup-Laubat and his arch-rival Camille Jenatzy went back and forth – each ending up with three records to their names. It was Jenatzy who had the final say.

As the new century dawned, the original record holder would have to contend with a very different kind of fight, this time against an illness that would, sadly, go on to claim his life in 1903.

RECORDS

Date	Speed	Place	Car
December 18, 1898	39.24mph	Achères, France	**Jeantaud Duc**
January 17, 1899	43.69mph	Achères, France	**Jeantaud Duc**
March 4, 1899	57.60mph	Achères, France	**Jeantaud Duc**

BELOW:
Chasseloup-Laubat, driving, with a
companion in 1885 – 13 years before his
record-breaking exploits. MPL

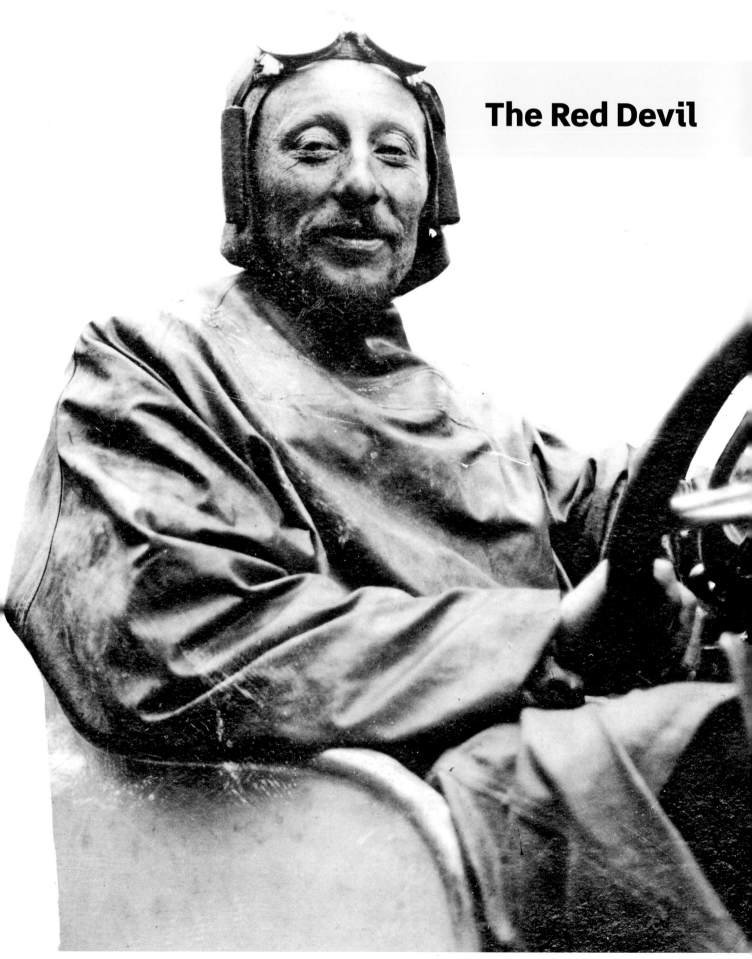

The Red Devil

Camille **Jenatzy**

LEFT:
Jenatzy at the
wheel. MPL

hen Belgian racer Camille Jenatzy heard of Chasseloup-Laubat's record-setting feat, he responded with a letter to La France Automobile in which he expressed disappointment at not being part of the original competition at Achères. He went on to challenge the Frenchman to a duel, and declared that under the same conditions he would defeat the Jeantaud.

The land speed record holder duly accepted, and the pair went head-to-head on January 17, 1899. Jenatzy, nicknamed Le Diable Rouge (The Red Devil) on account of his flowing ginger beard, became the first man to break the coveted mark by setting a speed of 41.42mph. However, his joy was short-lived as a mere 10 minutes later Chasseloup-Laubat claimed back the crown.

A fierce rivalry ensued, and conventional wisdom might have seen Jenatzy give up the fight when his nemesis clocked nearly 60mph in March of the same year, but the Belgian was undeterred. He returned with a modified electric machine and became the first man to drive at more than a mile per minute – a record that would remain unbroken for three years.

Jenatzy continued to race on tracks and roads across Europe, and piloted a Mercedes to victory in the highly sought-after Gordon Bennett Cup in Ireland in 1903 – subsequently offering a strange prediction that he would lose his life in the same make of car.

In a cruel twist of fate, his prophecy was realised in bizarre circumstances 10 years later. Hunting with friends in Luxemburg, he hid behind a tree and pretended to be an animal, a prank that worked far too well and led to another member of the party firing at him. Jenatzy was rushed to hospital, in a Mercedes, but bled to death before reaching a hospital.

■■ RECORDS			
Date	*Speed*	*Place*	*Car*
January 17, 1899	41.42mph	Achères, France	**CGA Dogcart**
January 27, 1899	49.92mph	Achères, France	**CGA Dogcart**
April 29, 1899	65.79mph	Achères, France	**La Jamais Contente**

RECORDS			
Date	*Speed*	*Place*	*Car*
April 13, 1902	75.06mph	Nice, France	**Gardner-Serpollet**

Léon **Serpollet**
Engineering excellence

Throughout the history of the land speed record, several engineers have piloted their own creations to glory – Frenchman Léon Serpollet was the first.

Born in the eastern part of the country in 1858, Serpollet developed a passion for mechanical work and moved to Paris, where he opened his own factory. Initially he concentrated on producing steam-powered three-wheeled carriages, his creations capable of more than 20mph – an impressive feat in 1894.

Two years later he perfected the design of a flash boiler suitable for use in cars, and so began a journey that would see him become the third man to hold the coveted title of fastest car and driver combination on the planet.

First, however, Serpollet turned his talents to the railroads and used his new steam technology to upgrade outdated French steam locomotives. By 1902 he had refocused on four wheels and, financed by American industrialist Frank Gardner, modified a car capable of challenging Jenatzy's near three-year-old mark.

On April 13, 1902, Serpollet took the car, nicknamed Easter Egg, on to the Promenade des Anglais in Nice, where he clocked more than 75mph over the flying kilometre. A new land speed record had been set.

LEFT:
Serpollet, with his wife as passenger, drives his Easter Egg steam car through the English seaside town of Bexhill in 1902. MPL

LAND SPEED PIONEERS

The concept of going fast is a relatively modern phenomenon. Steam engines on the railways took centre stage first, and as they developed and then found reliability in the mid-to-late 19th century it became apparent that speeds in excess of 30mph and 40mph were possible. In fact, as early as 1854 it's reported that a British train hit 81.80mph in Somerset; there's also evidence of a French locomotive travelling at 89.48mph in the north-east of the country in 1894.

While there are certainly questions to be asked about the accuracy of the timings, the stories of these mammoth achievements did make sure of two things: by the close of the century rates of 55mph to 60mph were now well within range, and any myths that still existed about the suffocating effect of speed on the human body had been well and truly shattered.

Less than 100 years prior, even the term 'miles per hour' would have had little meaning in the countries where these impressive efforts were being made. Now it

was the all-important benchmark, and it soon extended into other fields of engineering such as the advances being made in the development of the motor car.

German engineer Karl Benz introduced the first petrol-powered automobile in 1886, and it proved to be a huge leap forward. Various incarnations of steam and electric cars already existed, but they were made for comfort and convenience and not for speed. The internal combustion engine changed the industry.

As the number of cars swiftly multiplied, speed became the ultimate measure of performance. Whether it was the early drivers wanting to push the boundaries, or fascinated onlookers thrilled by the spectacle of these horseless carriages roaring past in a blur, people wanted to know just how fast cars could go.

The interest led to competition. Respective proponents of steam, electric and petrol wanted to prove that their power was better than the other. On top of that, each wanted to go faster than any other car had gone before.

LEFT: The Gordon Bennett Trophy was awarded to winners of the most prestigious races in the early days of motor sport. It was these events that gave an inkling into the speeds cars might be capable of reaching. ✪

Chasseloup-Laubat is pictured on March 4, 1899. On this date, in the electric Jeantaud Duc, the Frenchman set his third and final land speed record of 57.65mph. ✪

IN THE BEGINNING

How do you identify the fastest car? That was the question that industry titans, excited drivers and a curious public were asking as the new century came into view, and the early road races gave the first clear indications of what might be possible on four wheels.

These epic city-to-city battles weren't intended to reward speed, however. Of course it was pivotal, but road races covered hundreds of miles with the winner being the first driver to cross the finish line. Reliability and endurance (of both car and driver) were the two crucial qualities, and it meant the vehicles were never designed or tailored for optimum acceleration or velocity.

Still, by 1897 – three years after the first road race event had been established – the Paris-Amsterdam competition was won with an average speed of 26.9mph including all stops. The statistic was only worked out at the end, dividing the distance travelled by the time taken, and no speeds were measured en route. But it can surely be deduced that such a mark makes it almost impossible for the driver not to have exceeded 30mph, and perhaps he'd even touched 40mph, maybe 50mph.

Perhaps was not good enough, and it became clear that dedicated speed tests would bring enough interest from teams, drivers and spectators to be commercially viable. As one of the founders of the Automobile Club de France (ACF), M Paul Meyan was one such businessman to grasp the opportunity. He convinced his co-owners at respected motoring journal La France Automobile to sponsor a speed hill-climb held in the outskirts of Paris; an event, as it turned out, that

led directly to the creation of what's become known as the land speed record.

The November 27 hill-climb was hugely popular, and attracted a field of 47 entrants. Despite the impact of petrol power on the industry, it was electric that won the day as the Belgian Camille Jenatzy made the fastest ascent at 18mph.

Among the field was Gaston de Chasseloup-Laubat, a native of France who was also one of the ACF's founders. Technical issues had blighted his campaign, but he would have a chance of redemption on December 18 as La France Automobile announced a special sprint event 'at the request of one of our friends'.

Chasseloup-Laubat was the first entrant. He certainly fitted the bill as one of the publication's 'friends', and he began preparing his electric Jeantud Duc so he could demonstrate its capabilities across a smooth and level stretch of road in Archères that had been selected for this unique competition.

The journal declared that the sprint would determine the fastest driver and car combination in the world, and the ACF's involvement meant the winner would be accepted as such. Entries were plentiful, and so too was the viewing public, with numbers in the crowd exceeding 300.

A special 2000-metre course had been laid out; one kilometre for the standing start and then a further kilometre for the flying start. The

highest speed achieved overall would go into the history books.

Disappointingly for the competition, and for him personally, Jenatzy was at home and unable to attend. The two heavyweights would not go head to head, and in fact Chasseloup-Laubat's would be the only electric car in the field.

Internal combustion may well have been the future when it came to raw strength, but efficient delivery of the horsepower throughout the vehicle had yet to be perfected. As he lined up with his petrol-powered foes, Chasseloup-Laubat eased off the line ahead of the rest – and stayed there.

He completed the flying kilometre in 57 seconds to post the world's first official land speed record of 39.24mph. While that effort has become highly significant as the first entry in the grand history of the annals of outright land speed, even at the time it was considered rather tame. The thunderous steam trains of the day were far, far faster; and to add further context it must be remembered that the contemporary cycling record through the kilometre was only one second slower.

Still, the question of who and what was fastest had been answered, and a target set. For many, including Jenatzy, it felt like a target that was very much in reach.

Jenatzy responded to Chasseloup-Laubat's underwhelming victory by issuing a challenge; under the same course conditions and with a month to prepare he would set a higher speed. On January 17, 1899, the duo prepared for combat at the same course in Archères.

A fundamental reason why the Frenchman had been unable to extract something more spectacular from his Jeantaud was that he made almost no modifications for the task at hand. Its batteries (although responsible for its significant power) were heavier than standard engines of the day, and there was no effort to streamline the box-like front that was designed for touring and not sprinting.

It seemed Jenatzy had not realised the benefits of some fine-tuning either, and arrived with a similarly boxy machine. The challenger had the first run and, despite the obvious weaknesses, stayed true to his word by posting a 54-second flying kilometre – becoming the first man to break the land speed record and set in motion a classic duel.

That duel continued a mere 10 minutes later, Chasseloup-Laubat roaring back with a 51.2-second run to claim back his crown and improve the overall fastest speed to 43.69mph. It was good, but there was still a consensus that faster was possible – Jeantaud's motor having burned out in the final 200 metres demonstrating the fact.

Meyan's reporting of the frenzied back-and-forth was captivating his readers, and he had plenty of material to work with given that Jenatzy returned to Archères 10 days later on

The great Belgian racer celebrates becoming the second holder of the land speed record. ✪

Jenatzy sits proudly in La Jamais Contente as he prepares for a land speed record run. MPL

January 28 and lifted the record to just short of 50mph. The speeds might not have been phenomenal, but it was a thrilling head-to-head in the pursuit of glory. Each man had two records to his name, and there was still more to come.

The numbers may've been increasing, but with every run the great competitors were finally developing a deeper understanding of the internal mechanics and external factors which were influencing their ability to push ever faster. Chasseloup-Laubat was determined to win the record back for the Jeantaud marque and, after one unsuccessful attempt in February, he returned in March with a noticeably different machine.

Each of its wheels were now equal in size, the bodywork had been streamlined and it featured a new nose that cut through the air. Clearly the changes had worked, as the original record-holder lowered the world's top land speed by a remarkable six seconds to 57.6mph.

The motoring world was abuzz with the news and, after what had proved to be a rather limp start to the world's top land speed contest, the runs were now delivering the sorts of mind-boggling runs excited enthusiasts were expecting. If Chasseloup-Laubat had caused a stir, Jenatzy's reply was simply sensational.

Having been consistently one-upped by his rival since his much-publicised challenge, Jenatzy had focused the efforts of his own company on building a new car designed

specifically for the task in hand – the first in a long series of speed specials.

At the time the tyres were the thickest ever produced, the streamlined chassis was mirrored at the front and back and the two electric motors turned at a huge 900rpm. The 'freak' creation was named La Jamais Contente or 'The Never Satisfied' – an apt description of Jenatzy's relentless attitude to his epic battle.

On April 1, 1899, and with the adrenaline flowing, the Belgian powered off the line – once again at Archères – and roared through the flying kilometre. However, such was his eagerness, he'd set off before the timekeepers could get into position – there was no record this time.

Jenatzy was convinced he'd gone faster, and 28 days later he made no mistakes as he shaved more than four seconds from the top time and set a blistering average speed of 65.79mph. It was the first land speed record to surpass 100kph, a significant landmark in metric Europe.

La Jamais Contente had avenged defeat, and as it turned out Jenatzy had finally put the outright best out of Chasseloup-Laubat's reach. After an intense six-month period, the sixth and final record the pair exchanged would last for three years but by that time the insurmountable obstacle of heavy batteries had rendered electric cars obsolete against steam and petrol power.

Serpollet prepares his famous Easter Egg at Nice ahead of the annual speed trial during which he'll set a new top speed. ✪

At Bexhill in England, Serpollet shows what his Easter Egg can do. MPL

The concept of establishing the fastest car and driver in the world had come from the significant developments in the automotive industry, particularly the introduction of the internal combustion engine. Everyone wanted to know what type of car was fastest; electric had dominated early, and before petrol would get in on the act it was the turn of steam to make history.

By 1902, two of the era's top petrol racing cars had been taken agonisingly close to bettering Jenatzy's record – one of them had in fact equalled the mark, but the rules state that equal is not better. For both marques, Mors and Mercedes, glory would come later. But before it arrived, Frenchman Lèon Serpollet smashed the existing record at Nice Speed Week by breezing through the flying kilometre at a speed of 75.06mph – some 9mph faster than the Belgian.

Serpollet had proved himself as one of the world's finest makers of steam cars. One of his major breakthroughs was the invention of the flash boiler – a component that produces superhot steam by passing water through a heated coiled tube.

The annual Speed Week on France's south coast became one of the most important dates on the calendar in the early days of motor racing, and Serpollet had used the event to upstage the manufacturing giants of the time in the prestigious Rothschild Cup – the name of the speed trial held on the iconic Promenade des Anglais.

In 1901 he beat the premier Mercedes machines by a dominant six seconds, although ultimately fell short of the land speed record by 3mph. On April 13 the following year he took a four-cylinder creation out on to the course, housing a single-acting steam unit that turned at 1220rpm. He produced three of these sprint steamers between 1901 and 1903, the second and third named Easter Egg owing to their rounded profiles and because Speed Week was usually held around the Easter break.

It was the third incarnation Serpollet claimed to have used at Nice as he blasted down the course to become the third holder of the land speed record. It's noted in reports of the day that once through the timing trap it took another kilometre for Easter Egg to come to a stop, and it's incredible to think that the driver reached such speeds knowing his only way of braking was to shut down the engine.

Steam might have won a victory at Nice, but the increasing competitiveness in road racing meant far more powerful petrol engines were being produced. Serpollet decided to concentrate his time and resources on the commercial production side of his Gardner-Serpollet business, but he did so content with the knowledge that his name would forever be in the history books.

One of the top steam manufacturers, Serpollet realised petrol would dominate the LSR scene and so turned his attentions to his business. This Gardner-Serpollet steamer was one of the popular models in the company's range. MPL

William K **Vanderbilt**
The first American

ABOVE:
Willie K, the first American to become holder of the land speed record, doing what he loved most. Library of Congress ☉

illiam K
Vanderbilt
was the
grandson of William Henry Vanderbilt –
a railroad industry pioneer and one of
America's wealthiest individuals of the late
19th century.

Born into a life of luxury, Willie K – as
he was affectionately known – travelled
extensively as a child and teenager.
Europe, and France in particular, was one
such destination where the Vanderbilts
enjoyed spending their leisure time, and
it was during these frequent trips that the
youngster fell in love with motorsport.

Along with his brother, once he
reached adulthood he moved to Europe
to pursue his passion and joined French
road racing company Mors to challenge
the greats of the day. Realising that
Mors's new vehicles, powered by an
internal combustion engine, had the
potential to outpace the electric- and
steam-propelled machines of the previous
century, Vanderbilt soon set his sights on
conquering the land speed record.

In 1902 Émile Mors personally handed
over one of his prime racing cars for
Vanderbilt's assault, and with a few
minor modifications the American raised
Serpollet's effort by a mere 1.1mph to
become the first non-European holder of
the coveted title.

While it was a remarkable effort, it had
been achieved in a vehicle designed for
the roads and not straight-line speed. The
Mors was carrying brake, suspension and
steering equipment that was superfluous
to a straight speed run and amounted to
significant extra weight. It didn't take long
for others to catch on, and the ultimate
speed record was broken twice more that
year.

Two years later, Willie K attempted to
reclaim his crown and bring the title back
to America with a run on Daytona Beach
in Florida. Aboard a Mercedes, he covered
the flying mile in 39 seconds at 92.3mph
– more than 7mph faster than the existing
mark. Much to Vanderbilt's chagrin, the
racing establishment in Europe refused to
recognise the authenticity of the effort and
it failed to become an official land speed
record; although it's generally been
recognised as part of LSR history since.

RECORDS			
Date	Speed	Place	Car
August 5, 1902	76.08mph	Ablis, France	Mors

RECORDS

Date	Speed	Place	Car
November 5, 1902	76.60mph	Dourdan, France	**Mors**

Henri **Fournier**
Experienced professional

eing born in Le Mans, perhaps Henri Fournier was destined to become a success in the world of motorsport. As one of his country's most successful racing drivers – on two, three and four wheels – as well as briefly being a land speed record holder, he achieved exactly that. Beginning his career on motorcycles and tricycles, he joined the Mors automobile team in 1901 and quickly became one of their most prominent drivers by winning both the Paris-Bordeaux and Paris-Berlin races. As well as his success on the roads, Fournier was noted for his ability in speed tests and held several of Mors's own records. He also showed his talents at the 1902 Paris-Vienna race by setting an average speed of more than 70mph on the first leg – a dominant performance that would most likely have led to victory if not for a mechanical failure.

After Vanderbilt had become the land speed record holder in August of the same year, Fournier was one of those to believe the effort could be bettered with some relatively simple modifications to the same Mors model driven by the American. In early November, Fournier fractionally lifted the top speed to 76.6mph – a target that was overhauled just 12 days later. Having initially retired, Fournier returned to racing later in his career while also becoming a car dealer. Together with his brother, he went on to create Établissements Fournier and became a manufacturer.

LEFT:
Fournier, the driver, is pictured at the French Grand Prix in 1914 – 12 years after his record-breaking exploits. ✪

Maurice **Augières**
The unheralded amateur

There is little information to be found about the life and times of Mors's third and final record holder, and perhaps that's to be expected given that he was an amateur within the team's ranks.

The driver in question was a Parisian merchant named Maurice Augières, and despite being a relative novice he became the land speed record holder with a run of 77.13mph in 1902.

Much to the disgust of the distinguished Fournier, the new mark was set less than a fortnight after his own successful effort – and was achieved in exactly the same car over exactly the same stretch of road.

Each of the Mors trio had only managed to shave mere fractions from the previous highest speed, but they had entered the record books nonetheless and in doing so had established the internal combustion engine as the new powerplant of choice for record attempts.

It was still evident, however, that road-going vehicles could be further adapted for straight-line speed and within just a couple of years the land speed record would be edging ever closer to 100mph.

RIGHT:

Not a great deal is known about Augières, and it's believed that there are no pictures of him in common existence. This shot, from Bexhill in the English county of East Sussex, shows the 1902 Mors – the same type of car in which the amateur French competitor shocked the established drivers of the day to become the land speed record holder.

RECORDS

Date	Speed	Place	Car
November 17, 1902	77.13mph	Dourdan, France	**Mors**

RECORDS			
Date	*Speed*	*Place*	*Car*
July 17, 1903	83.47mph	Ostend, Belgium	**Gobron-Brillié**
November 5, 1903	84.73mph	Dourdan, France	**Gobron-Brillié**

ABOVE:
The Gobron-Brillié was rather ungainly, but undoubtedly fast. Here, Duray is pictured preparing for action at a 1903 speed trial in Nice, France. MPL

ith the development of the internal combustion engine came increasing competitiveness in the realm of motor racing, particularly on the roads. Mors had established itself as a major name, but there were many others; one such manufacturer seeking success was Paris-based Gobron-Brillié.

In pursuit of improved performance for races came bigger engines and increased efficiency, and the obvious by-product of this development was faster cars. While these weren't being produced with the sole focus of breaking the land speed record, they were clearly capable of doing so.

Gobron-Brillié's driver Arthur Duray demonstrated this during a speed trial at Ostend, in his native Belgium,

Arthur **Duray**　　　**At the double**

in July 1903. The flying kilometre was conquered in just 26.8 seconds – a speed of 83.47mph – a dominant performance that increased the previous best by more than 5mph. Wrestling the record from Mors was a feather in the cap of Duray and Gobron-Brillié, but both driver and team were well aware that it was possible to go even faster.

Later in the year the combination had another crack,

this time at Dourdan where all three of the Mors drivers had achieved history, and Duray managed to raise the bar even further to 84.73mph.

While Gobron-Brillié was far from finished, Duray's second record would prove to be his last. Born in 1882, he was a still a relative youngster however, and continued to find success in his racing career into the mid-1930s.

PETROL COMES TO THE FORE

There was a general acceptance in the early era of racing that the internal combustion engine was the future of speed. But despite the premier outfits of the time deploying petrol power, it was electric and then steam that shared the first seven land speed records.

It's difficult to pinpoint exactly why it took so long for this dominant form in road racing to establish a similar superiority in speed trials. Internal combustion was perhaps more complex, requiring a number of different parts and components to work in harmony as it powered vehicles through the flying kilometre.

It had been three years since Jenatzy's third and final land speed record, and there was a feeling throughout the racing fraternity that it was time to end the reign. Once the premier petrol-engine manufacturers and their drivers caught up, it seemed there would be no stopping them and an incredible period was about to commence. During the course of the next seven remarkable years the outright top speed would be raised 16 times.

The first to have a crack was Englishman Charles Stewart Rolls, he who would go on to become one of motoring's most famous names alongside Frederick Henry Royce. However, in 1902 it wasn't the luxury British brand he had at his disposal but instead a 60hp, 9.2-litre, four-cylinder beast developed and prepared by pioneering French factory Mors.

Alongside Panhard et Levassor, Mors dominated the early days of automobile racing and was one of the first companies to utilise the V-engine configuration – generally making its powerplants smaller and lighter, excellent qualities in the pursuit of increased velocity. Its use of pneumatic shock absorbers aimed at reducing spring rebound was also a novel addition to the large racing vehicles of the early 20th century.

Unfortunately for Rolls he was not one of the successful competitors, and having gone to Archères set on overhauling Jenatzy he ultimately came up 2mph short. Another petrol contender soon emerged in the

form of American millionaire William K Vanderbilt, who had used his fortune to purchase both a new Mors 60 and the latest Mercedes-Simplex 40. The latter of these was an upgrade of the German giant's first incarnation that introduced the world to the unforgettable pressed steel chassis and honeycomb radiator.

Once again Archères was selected as the course, and Vanderbilt came agonisingly close to greatness as the Mercedes powered to 65.79mph to exactly match Jenatzy. Petrol was getting closer, but still wasn't quite good enough. While focus at this point was on the car – and clearly the weapon at hand was the decisive factor – would-be record-holders also began to consider location. All LSR attempts had so far been at Archères and, while the ACF wanted as much consistency as possible to avoid discrepancies, a thought emerged that course conditions could have a significant impact.

Serpollet went some way to proving this when he upset the applecart at Nice, just as it seemed certain that the next fastest car would be powered by petrol. His steaming behemoth would probably have gone just as fast (faster than Jenatzy at least) had he made his run at Archères, but it certainly opened up the possibility of going in search of the absolute ideal conditions in order to extract those few crucial miles per hour more.

ABOVE: William K Vanderbilt readies his Mors for a record-breaking run, the first made by a petrol-powered car. ✿

FOURNIER ON THE "MORS" MACHINE WITH WHICH HE WON THE PARIS-BORDEAUX AND PARIS-BERLIN RACES AND BEAT THE VANDERBILT RECORD FOR ONE KILOMETRE.

MORS MAKES ITS MARK

Sure that either his Mors or the Mercedes – or perhaps even both – were capable of going faster than the steam king Serpollet, Vanderbilt was the first to explore his options. By the end of the same April the new record had been set, the American had twice attempted and twice failed to beat the existing best – both at different courses.

The first effort came on the road between Chartres and Bonneval, south-west of Paris, where he posted 67.78mph in the Mercedes during a one-on-one battle with fellow millionaire motoring enthusiast Henri de Rothschild. Joined by yet another wealthy American, Wolf Bishop, the series moved to a stretch further south, outside Ablis and St Arnoult, where once again it was Vanderbilt setting the pace. Again, however, he

couldn't match Serpollet, although he did achieve the fastest recorded speed for a petrol car at 69.04mph. He was getting closer.

It was a Mors driver who would be the first to genuinely threaten though, as the Belgian baron Pierre de Caters took his 60hp Paris-Vienna race-winning machine to a speed trial in his home country and equalled Serpollet. Petrol had reached the top at last, albeit not alone and officially, as it had matched and not defeated.

The determined and well-financed Vanderbilt refused to relent, and returned to the Ablis-St Arnoult road on August 5 and this time he switched to his Mors. Bursting off the line to a cacophony of engine roars, and amid a cloud of fumes, he smashed through the flying kilometre in 29.4 seconds to finally set an undisputed and outright

petrol-powered land speed record more than three-and-a-half years since the competition had been conceived.

Vanderbilt rejoiced, and so did Mors – being able to boast the fastest car in the world among its range was a huge sales and marketing advantage, even in the days before these concepts had been fully formed. Having captured

One of Mors's premier drivers, Fournier was determined to capture the land speed record for himself, his employer and his country. He was successful, although his tenure lasted just two weeks. He went on to even greater success, however, and is shown competing in the 1911 French GP at Le Mans. ✪

Augières might have been an amateur, but he did have experience – pictured here during the 1903 Paris-Madrid race. ⊙

the record, the American's LSR love affair was over for the time being; Mors however would have two more records before the year was out.

Henri Fournier was the famed French professional driver and was considered as one of the greats, given his victories in the Paris-Bordeaux and Paris-Berlin races of 1901. On learning about Vanderbilt's exploits, Fournier reasoned that if an amateur could achieve such a speed with a French Mors, then a French champion could do better.

On yet another new course at Dourdan, in the north of France,

Fournier backed up his bold claims – although only just. With little in the way of build-up that had accompanied Vanderbilt's runs, he arrived at the course on November 5 and shaved one-fifth of a second off the time through the flying kilometre, lifting the land speed record to 76.60mph.

The ACF determined that Dourdan provided the perfect all-round conditions for its competition, and determined that it should become the official course for attempts on the outright top speed. It never really caught on as a policy, but it did become the venue for the next

record-breaking run that occurred just a fortnight later.

Behind the wheel on that occasion was unknown Paris merchant and amateur driver Maurice Augières, who had been able to negotiate the loan of a factory Mors. Much to the disgust of an incredulous Fournier, Augières covered the required distance in 29 seconds exactly for a new land speed record of 77.13mph.

It proved to be a fascinating period as petrol battled steam, amateurs took on professionals and the major marques staked claims to being the fastest manufacturer in the market. Throughout the heated head-to-heads however, the actual numbers were only being increased by just a few miles per hour at a time – sometimes by mere fractions. Petrol had established itself as the preferred power, and Mors as the top team, but no one had established any real dominance.

That was about to change.

LEFT: Land speed record cars and drivers were proving their credentials in various timed events, particularly in popular hill climbs. Mors's Augières did just that in the 1902 Chateau-Thierry competition in Paris, just a few months before his LSR exploits. ⊙

In July 1903, Arthur Duray lined up at the start of a speed trial held just outside the coastal town of Ostend in his native Belgium.

Under his command sat a rather large and ungainly monster in the form of the 13.5-litre Gobron-Brillié, a powerful model from the Paris-based manufacturer that housed a four-cylinder, 110hp engine using opposed pistons. This new type of design, while sizeable, eliminated the need for a heavy cylinder head. It was a complex production but, along with the reduced weight, its main benefits were that it cut the workload of the pistons at high speed and removed vibrations.

These characteristics made it ideal for travelling long distances, and it was also extremely effective once it had passed through a relatively cumbersome period of acceleration. It wasn't likely to set the world alight from a standing start, but through the flying kilometre it had the makings of a feared competitor. And so it proved to be when the flag dropped.

After a calm and unremarkable start, Duray moved through the gears with ease to complete the course in just 26.8 seconds – a speed of 83.47mph and a resounding new land speed record. Just to emphasise the Gobron-Brillié's capabilities, a similar car driven by Louis Rigolly

Duray prepares for action at the 1912 French GP, on board an Alcyon. ○

was runner-up and both vehicles were victorious in several more timed hill-climbs during the summer.

Mors was immediately desperate to regain its crown and on two occasions believed it had, only to be denied by the authorities at the ACF. First it was Rolls who appeared back on the scene, and this time he had the 70hp Dauphin model to play with – a car that had conquered all in its path during the 1903 Paris-Madrid race.

The Englishman took it to a private course on the Duke of Portland's estate in Clipstone near Nottinghamshire, and was timed by officials of the Automobile Club of Great Britain and Ireland as having passed through the flying kilometre faster than Duray at a speed of 84.73mph. Rolls's effort was rejected officially by the ACF because 'approved timing apparatus' had not

been used, and probably also owing to the stretch of road having a definite decline. Another Mors fanatic, Maurice de Forest, also ran into the issue of approved timing when he reduced Duray's time by a fifth of a second during the Irish Speed Fortnight in Dublin.

It would certainly not be the final time that the arbiters of the land speed record refused to approve a timed record run, and while it did create debate and uncertainty it also served to maintain consistent conditions, ensuring driver and car were the only variables when in pursuit of perfection. What it's also done is to make the evolution of the record far more up and down than the tidy straight line that it should really be – but more on that later.

The two speeds achieved by Rolls and de Forest might not have been official, but Duray had clearly taken note of the Dauphin Mors. He took the lusty Gobron-Brillié to the ACF's preferred course at Dourdan in a bid to put his rivals out of sight, but after multiple attempts he could only match what Rolls had done rather than surpass it.

Given the Briton's effort had not been accepted, Duray had beaten his own existing best and therefore set a land speed record – a second for both him and the team. It was November 17, and although he might have wanted to beat Rolls and attempt the first-ever 140kph, it was time to break for the winter. The Belgian went home having just about put Mors in its place.

LEFT: Clearly quite a character, Duray – with his land speed record more than a decade behind him – works on his machine at the 1914 French GP. ○

Louis **Rigolly**
Bringing up the ton

There were times during the early 1900s when it seemed as if the land speed record was broken on a monthly basis.

Whether it be engineers, race drivers, amateur hopefuls or businessmen, a group of ambitious individuals quickly wrote themselves into the record books – but Louis Rigolly will always have a special place in the story as the first driver to break the 100mph mark.

It took the Frenchman two attempts to get there, although his first effort of 94.78mph at Nice in March 1904 also proved to be a record-breaker as he extended Gobron-Brillié's dominance over its rivals.

While that speed would be bettered just two months later, Rigolly was not finished and made a series of modifications to the car's streamlining. He took the Gobron-Brillié to Ostend, where Duray had proved the manufacturer's credentials, and he roared across the sand at an incredible 103.56mph to claim back his title.

Like many of his contemporaries in pursuit of high-speed glory, Rigolly's main endeavour was road racing and both before and after his LSR exploits he was a successful competitor in the Grand Prix events of the day.

RIGHT:
Rigolly, the first land speed record holder to surpass 100mph, pictured in 1904. MPL

RECORDS			
Date	Speed	Place	Car
March 31, 1904	94.78mph	Nice, France	**Gobron-Brillié**
July 21, 1904	103.56mph	Ostend, Belgium	**Gobron-Brillié**

Pierre de **Caters**
The Belgian aviator

RECORDS

Date	Speed	Place	Car
May 25, 1904	97.25mph	Ostend, Belgium	**DMG Mercedes Simplex**

andwiched between Rigolly's two land speed record runs was a 97.25mph blast down the sand at Ostend by Belgian aviation pioneer Baron Pierre de Caters. Among the road racers who launched attempts to set the fastest speed ever recorded, de Caters was somewhat of an anomaly.

Yes, he was a motor racing competitor, but a little like William K Vanderbilt his interests spread further and wider than four wheels and he was renowned as an adventurer, aviator and motorboat racer.

In the years after short tenure as holder of the LSR title he became the first Belgian to receive a pilot licence in 1909, was the first Belgian aircraft manufacturer and the first instructor of military aviation in his country.

LEFT:
Understood to be the gentleman at the centre of the group, the baron is pictured in 1904 with his record-breaking Mercedes. MPL

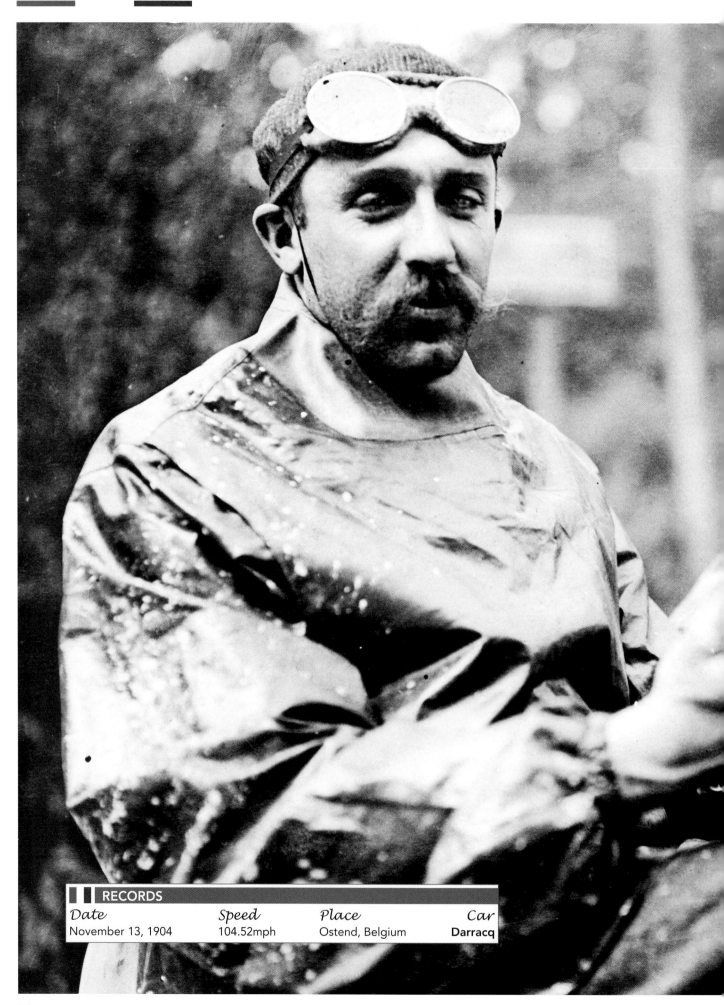

RECORDS

Date	Speed	Place	Car
November 13, 1904	104.52mph	Ostend, Belgium	**Darracq**

Paul **Baras**
Darracq has its day

Racing outfits Mors and Gobron-Brillié had made their respective marks on the land speed record, and in late 1904 it was time for another French team in the form of Darracq to get involved.

One of its drivers, Paul Baras, had been challenging Rigolly and de Caters throughout the year but had been unable to match his rivals both in speed runs and in the longer road races. Not to be deterred, Darracq moved a convoy of cars and drivers to Ostend for a sustained assault on Rigolly's new best effort, and the result was Baras completing the flying kilometre in 21.4 seconds – a new record of 104.52mph.

The following year saw a definitive shift away from road-going vehicles to specially created speed machines, and so Baras became the last of the road racers (driving road-racing cars) to claim the ultimate prize.

In 1906 the Frenchman finished seventh in the inaugural French Grand Prix, setting the fastest lap of the race in the process, before getting on the podium a year later after coming home in third.

LEFT:
Baras, in 1904, at the wheel of his
Darracq. MPL

CONTROVERSY, CHAOS AND THE MAGICAL TON

A fascinating, and equally complex, period followed Duray's double as the land speed record scene demonstrated the wonderful highs and farcical lows it's seemed capable of producing in its long history.

The eventful year – January 1904 through to January 1905 – began and ended with the record in dispute as four seemingly legitimate claims set on American soil were flatly rejected for entry into the record books

by the ACF. In between, however, Frenchman Louis Rigolly had officially and unquestionably become the first man to break the much-vaunted 100mph mark in a highly memorable and historic run at Ostend on July 21.

To help clarify matters, the timeline below provides an overview of back-and-forth that occurred during those incredible 12 months – the subsequent three pages uncovers the story.

RECORDS TIMELINE

	Date	Speed	Driver	Place
UNOFFICIAL	January 12, 1904	91.37mph	Henry Ford	Lake St Clair, USA
UNOFFICIAL	January 27, 1904	92.30mph	William K Vanderbilt	Daytona Beach, USA
OFFICIAL	March 31, 1904	94.78mph	Louis Rigolly	Nice, France
OFFICIAL	May 25, 1904	97.25mph	Pierre de Caters	Ostend, Belgium
OFFICIAL	July 21, 1904	103.55mph	Louis Rigolly	Ostend, Belgium
OFFICIAL	November 13, 1904	104.52mph	Paul Baras	Ostend, Belgium
UNOFFICIAL	January 25, 1905	104.65mph	Arthur MacDonald	Daytona Beach, USA
UNOFFICIAL	January 25, 1905	109.75mph	Herbert Bowden	Daytona Beach, USA

The Gobron-Brillié was pure muscle, and one of the great land speed record cars. Rigolly is in the driver's seat here.
MPL

THE OFFICIAL RECORD-BREAKERS

Glory for Rigolly came in 1904, but he'd attempted to break the record before in this less refined Gobron-Brillié at the ACF's 'official' Dourdan course. ✪

The Belgian de Caters is pictured in 1902 driving a Mors, an image captured before his switch to Mercedes where he found land speed record success. ✪

While plenty of 'unofficial' LSR activity was occurring across the Atlantic, in Europe the season kicked off with Nice Speed Week. Gobron-Brillié was still the team to beat – according to the record books it still held the top outright effort – and it also had a point to prove given that it was facing challenges from the United States.

The Parisian outfit clearly had no intention of squabbling over which record had most authority; instead it sent out an improved 130hp, 13.6-litre model with the intention of defeating any potential challenge, unofficial or otherwise.

With no real attempt at streamlining, and knowing the Promenade des Anglais was becoming unsuitable for the higher speeds now being achieved, driver Louis Rigolly would have to rely on raw power – the Gobron-Brillié had it in spades. He'd also have to demonstrate considerable skill, something he did not lack.

On witnessing the monster machine roar down the course, one motoring journalist reported: "Rigolly's car, marvellously controlled, was upon us with a low rumble, seeming scarce to touch the ground but rather as if balanced above it. The meteor crossed the finishing line, we were drowned in dust. There was an explosion of surprise and joy when the timekeepers announced an unbelievable 152.54kph for the flying kilometre." Rigolly had offered a stunning retort to the 'American pretenders', and there were more lining up to do the same.

It was Mercedes that struck first as perennial challenger Pierre de Caters went within a whisper of 100mph at

Ostend on May 25 to win the outright speed back for the German firm. Clocking 97.25mph, he claimed he'd had a crack at the record just to "annoy Panhard, Mors and Gobron-Brillié a little". It might not have been the best idea as one of his rivals bit back emphatically.

Rigolly took his trusted steed to Belgium for the July speed trials, held at the same venue as de Caters's record run. It was here that Gobron-Brillié first went into battle with Paul Baras and his Darracq. The new manufacturer on the scene was making noise in sprint and hill-climb events – although it was failing miserably in road races – and its new model arrived as a genuine challenger.

Design was bold and innovative; it boasted an 11.3-litre, four-cylinder powerplant, as well as advanced bodywork with enclosed sides and shaft drive at a time when chains were believed to be pivotal for high-speed vehicles. Clearly Darracq and Baras had got it right, and had it not been for Rigolly's heroics the car and driver combination would have left with a

new land speed record as they finished just two-fifths of a second behind their rival. As it was, pure horsepower won the day. The Frenchman and the Gobron-Brillié flew across the course in 21.6 seconds for a new outright best of 103.55mph. The once unthinkable speed of 100mph had been achieved.

The Darracq was to have its day, however, and it came just four months later as the team took a range of vehicles to Ostend for an assault on a variety of speed records. Each resulted in success, the final run yielding an average speed of 104.52mph for Baras across the flying kilometre, taking him ahead of Rigolly. There were murmurings of surprise that a car not capable of 100mph in July could now go close to 105mph – and a story did the rounds that one crucial kilometre marker was moved in the Darracq's favour.

Whatever the truth, Baras officially held the land speed record for more than a year. Unofficially it was defeated swiftly by at least one, possibly two, entries at the 1905 Florida Speed Week.

Baras was a star attraction at Grand Prix events such as this one in France in 1908. Not only was he a racing great of the era, but he could boast a land speed record to his name. ✪

THE UNOFFICIAL CONTENDERS

The motor car industry was growing as quickly in America as it was in Europe and Henry Ford, founder of the now iconic Ford company, wanted a piece of the land speed action to help promote his new brand across the country. His eagerness led to the first attempt at the land speed record to occur in the USA – a country that would later become its home.

January 12, 1904, was Ford's chosen date, being that it was a week before the New York Automobile Show where he was launching a new Model B and wanted to maximise publicity. The frozen Lake St Clair in Michigan, a small stretch of water in among the Great Lakes, was selected as the venue – the first and last time the land speed record was targeted on ice.

A mile-long course was set out, the American officials not even contemplating the concept of a kilometre marker, and Ford's Arrow bellowed off the line. He had chosen the frozen water because it guaranteed a dead-level track, but once he picked up speed he soon encountered

He would go on to become the world's most famous car-maker, and here Henry Ford stands next to his Ford 999 racer with American racer Barney Oldfield on board. This car was a twin to Arrow, the vehicle Ford would use for his unofficial land speed record run on the frozen waters of Lake St Clair in 1904. MPL

partially melted patches of ice and as he approached 90mph the car was leaping and bounding almost out of control.

It was an incredible performance from a man with little-to-no experience of high-speed driving, and as he came to a safe halt it all proved worthwhile as he beat Duray's figure by an impressive 7mph to post 91.37mph – it was a record that Ford claimed "went all over the world".

Unfortunately for the American, that was not the case. Timing for his run had been administered by the American Automobile Association, and the ACF didn't recognise the group as the ruling motoring authority in the USA so therefore the result was void. No one could dispute the figures, Ford had indeed gone as fast as he claimed, but it would not be an official land speed record.

LEFT: Vanderbilt claimed an unofficial land speed record in 1904, his second in total. He's pictured here during the 1908 Vanderbilt Cup, the first major trophy in American automobile racing and an international event he founded four years prior.✪

Unlike Rolls, or others who'd fallen foul of the French, Ford just simply ignored the decision. In his eyes, in American eyes, and in the eyes of many more around the world he had the fastest car and was the fastest driver. Or at least he was for just less than a fortnight.

Florida Speed Week had been inaugurated in 1903, and in its second year William K Vanderbilt arrived on the beach at Ormond-Daytona with a 90hp Mercedes intent on reclaiming the land speed record he'd held two years prior.Starting what would become a long affinity between the record and the Daytona course, Vanderbilt beat Ford's speed after just 13 days.

Yet again, the ACF was adamant that the outright best was still held by Duray – but there was widespread acceptance among the motoring community that indeed Ford and then Vanderbilt had legitimately captured the crown.Fortunately the impasse only lasted two months as Rigolly bested them both at Nice, but confusion would rear its head once again at the third annual American speed showpiece.

THE LAST ROAD-RACER

A British marque was next to enter the fray, as a Napier driven by Arthur MacDonald became the last road-racing car to contest the LSR. It shared many similarities with the Mercedes used by Vanderbilt, save for its unique six-cylinder engine that allowed for a sizable capacity of 15 litres. MacDonald put the additional power to good use at Daytona to win three trophies and set seven speed records, the most significant being a flying mile of 24.4 seconds – 104.65mph.

Depending on which set of governing rules are subscribed to the Napier, either it never held the record at all, or it and MacDonald were the outright fastest car and driver in the world for the next 12 months. Just to compound the unusual situation and highlight the disjointed nature of the LSR at this time, a third argument insisted that the British had been toppled within a matter of hours.

That's because before the Napier had even begun to cool, a custom-built Mercedes housing two 60hp engines made a sensational run of 109.75mph, leaving enthralled spectators and officials flabbergasted. It had been a breathless afternoon on the American east coast, but still the drama was not over as The Flying Dutchman – nicknamed as such by its creator and driver, the American Herbert Bowden – was disqualified for being over the 1000kg limit for sprint events.

There is no reason why its time still couldn't be considered by US officials for a land speed record where there was no such rule against maximum weight, but its run was considered void and therefore Bowden was not given a place in the record books.

Even if the Mercedes special had been entered, the overarching French authority was still refusing to acknowledge any supposed land speed record run to have taken place on American soil. The rigid ACF initially refused to budge, and for a time it seemed as if the prestigious title would peter out into a multitude of regional records. Thankfully the organisation saw sense, and at the 1906 Florida Speed Week competitors were able to cover the flying kilometre. If a world best time was achieved, it would become official.

The British Napier was the last racing machine designed for the road used to attempt a land speed record. Speeds had reached such a level that only specially created vehicles were now capable of challenging the outright top time. MPL

RECORDS

Date	Speed	Place	Car
December 30, 1905	109.65mph	Arles, France	**Darracq**
November 8, 1909	125.94mph	Brooklands, Great Britain	**Blitzen Benz**

Victor **Hémery**
Chief tester, top driver

et another Frenchman to have claimed the LSR crown, Victor Hémery was among the greatest competitors in the golden age of early motorsport. He first joined Darracq as its chief tester in 1904, but soon proved himself more than able behind the wheel as he claimed a string of race victories in Europe and the US. To add icing on the cake, in 1905 he piloted a Darracq special to a new land speed record of just less than 110mph.

As a multiple winner and holder of the world record, Hémery's talents were in demand and in 1907 he accepted an offer to join German team Benz. The move worked for all concerned as he claimed victory in the St Petersburg-Moscow road race in appalling conditions and then backed it up by taking podiums in the new French and US Grand Prix.

As if his achievements weren't enough to earn legendary status, four years after his first record-breaking run he recaptured the land speed record with a blistering 125.94mph effort in his new team's Blitzen Benz. And the victories didn't end there, continuing on into 1911 when he earned his final first-place finish at the French Grand Prix on his home track of Sarthe.

LEFT:

Victor Hémery was the first man to earn land speed records for two different teams, one of many impressive achievements during a glittering career. He's pictured here at the 1911 French Grand Prix, an event that yielded his final race victory. ✪

The FEARLESS FEW

RIGHT:
Marriott, in the light-coloured overalls, poses beachside in 1906 with the Stanley Steamer. MPL

RECORDS			
Date	Speed	Place	Car
January 26, 1906	121.57mph	Ormond Beach, USA	Stanley Steamer

By the mid-1910s petrol power was king when it came to the land speed record, and accepted wisdom was that steam would never again be capable of competing. The Stanley brothers of Boston, Massachusetts, had other ideas.

Their Stanley Steamer was an admirable performer in touring car competitions on both American and European roads, and they decided to further their

reputation by developing their product to be capable of taking on international speed records.

During the 1906 Florida speed week, with their compatriot Fred Marriott behind the wheel, the Stanleys realised a dream by seeing their vehicle reach an electrifying 121.57mph through the flying kilometre and an even more staggering 127.66mph across the mile. For reasons explored throughout these pages, the French

Fred **Marriott** Steam revival

authorities refused to recognise the higher mile speed, but did accept the lower mark as a land speed record.

While not being an official effort, Marriott's phenomenal speed has since been widely considered to be part of LSR history. In reaching such heights he became the first man to exceed 200kph and two miles per minute, and it also became the first time a car had beaten the top speed record of a train.

It also became the last land speed record achieved under steam power, and it was more than a century before another steam-driven vehicle went faster in a speed test – Charles Burnett took Inspiration to 139.84mph in California in 2009. Marriott had attempted to break his own record in 1907 on Daytona Beach, but hit a rut while travelling in excess of 120mph and crashed heavily. He immediately retired from speed trials.

RECORDS

Date	Speed	Place	Car
June 24, 1914	124.12mph	Brooklands, Great Britain	**Blitzen Benz**

Lydston **Hornsted**
New British interest

Born to a British diplomat and his wife in Russia, Lydston Hornsted eventually moved 'home' to the United Kingdom to work as a mechanic.

Like other record-breakers before him, his interest soon led to opportunities in the driver's seat, and by 1913 he was taking on various speed challenges for the Benz team he had joined.

After conquering both the standing-start half-mile and kilometre bests, he asked the Benz engineers to modify the car he'd used for an attempt at the top prize. Early in 1914 he broke more records over two miles and five miles, looking set to conquer the ultimate target with ease.

Despite having to adapt to new rule changes that saw attempts on the speed requiring two runs made in opposite directions with an average being taken, Hornsted became Britain's first holder of the land speed record in June 1914 with a figure of 124.12mph.

It would take eight years for Hornsted's effort to be bettered, although much of the hiatus in LSR attempts was due to the First World War that began mere months after his heroics at Brooklands.

LEFT:
The epitome of a true British gentleman, Hornsted held multiple speed records – including the big one. ✪

STEAM'S FINAL FLOURISH

Despite not being universally accepted as the world's fastest car, Bowden's incredible creation had demonstrated to would-be speed merchants that the days of the road-racer in speed trials were at an end. These bulky units, designed for endurance, were quite simply no longer fast enough to compete.

Claims from the Americans and British aside, Baras and his Darracq were still the official holders of the outright land speed crown and the manufacturer was desperate to hold on to its title. Alexandre Darracq himself realised time had come for change, and directed his engineer Louis Ribeyrolles to design a new 'special' capable of defeating all in its path.

The creator took two of the outfit's 160mm x 140mm four-cylinder blocks, converted the heads to full overhead valves, and mounted them at 90 degrees on a new type of crankcase. His work resulted in a 22.5-litre, 200hp, V8 beast, capable of turning at a breathtaking 1200rpm.

This incredible feat of automotive production turned out to be a precursor to the V8 powerplants found in the supercars of today, but in 1905 for Darracq it was housed in a small, wire-wheeled chassis with a wheelbase of just eight feet and six inches – the average road-racer was nearly a foot bigger. Bodywork was minimal – just two bucket seats on a nearly non-existent chassis, and total weight was a shade under 978kg. Such a slight frame with that power was potentially unbeatable.

Rushed straight from the factory in Paris to a long stretch of road between Arles and Salon near Marseilles, team driver Victor Hémery showed what it could do with a blistering run across the kilometre of 109.65mph – exactly 5mph faster than MacDonald's unofficial best, and by default better than Baras's mark, making it a new land speed record. It was December 30, 1905, and Hémery would go into the new year as a national hero.

As his countrymen rejoiced that he'd brought 'their' record home, Britain could have few complaints – the Darracq had bested the Napier fair and square. In the USA, however, there was still the not-insignificant matter of Bowden's 109.75mph.

France might not have been interested, but another American certainly was – and he was ready to take it on with a very 'special' car indeed.

Hémery in the Darracq, 1904. ✪

FRED MARRIOTT AND THE STANLEY ROCKET

Petrol exponents had it all their own way in the early 1900s, and for many the notion of steam or electric ever again challenging for the land speed record was inconceivable. They were on the money when it came to electric, but Serpollet had shown what steam could do when it came to raw power; it was about to shock the world once more.

Brothers Francis E and Freeland O Stanley of Massachusetts, USA, had won many admirers for their Stanley Steamer. As a tourer it had impressed in America and Europe, and then had shown its capabilities as a sprinter both on the sand at Daytona and in hill climbs. Given that it generated significant publicity, the siblings decided to dabble in record-breaking – aiming to enhance their already respected brand. And so in 1905 the Stanley Company got to work on a new record car.

The engine had just 15 moving parts, far less complex than its internal combustion cousins, and at just 185lb was remarkably light. A reinforced boiler was able to withstand pressure of up to 1000lb psi and was mounted ahead of the rear axle with the driver sat further forward. Bodywork resembled an upturned boat, and had been designed by boat-building company JR Robertson of Boston from thin cedar strips covered with canvas. Its clean lines and aerodynamic appearance was disturbed only by a brass funnel for the release of fumes. Attractive as this new breed of steam-powered automobile was, it had been carefully constructed to achieve maximum velocity. Total weight was a modest 740kg, and at full tick it was able to put out around 120hp at 800rpm; the power-to-weight ratio gave it every chance of being a serious contender.

American driver Fred Marriott

The beautifully shaped Stanley Rocket, with Marriott at the helm. ✪

was selected for the record-breaking campaign and, with no clutch or gear-changing as a distraction, his focus was to hold the baying beast still at the start line before firing away when boiler pressure had built to its maximum. The Stanley car was christened Rocket, apt given the violent nature of its take-off.

Marriott served notice of what was to come during practice at Daytona in January 1906 – a phenomenal run through the mile was timed at 30.6 seconds, a whopping 1.8 seconds faster than Bowden. One slight issue was that the Rocket's weight concentrated on its back wheels and so the front end had a tendency to lift. A modification to the front spring proved to be the final piece of the puzzle.

Darracq's V8, the official LSR champion, remained the Stanley's fiercest rival but it simply had no answer. Marriott broke five records and claimed five trophies to dominate his petrol-powered foes – much to their dismay. Louis Chevrolet, he of the Chevrolet Motor Car Company, had brief success in the Darracq and did indeed go through the flying kilometre in a record-breaking time of 19.4 seconds. Cruel, yet glorious, Marriott went straight out in the Stanley and shaved a full second off his fellow American's time to post a simply unfathomable 121.57mph. He, and not Chevrolet, finished the competition as the holder of the land speed record.

Less than 10 years earlier, the first outright best speed in the world was set at 39.24mph; now it stood at more than two miles per minute. To even greater astonishment, a rampant Marriott ran at 127.6mph in the flying mile competition. Proving that all was still not entirely at ease within the motoring fraternity, the mile speed was still not accepted by the authorities in France and so the record remained at the Stanley's kilometre run of 121.57. Still, steam was king once again and it was going to take

A feared competitor, the Stanley brothers' special faced no challengers the year after its 1906 record-breaking run and so set about extending its own best speed. Unfortunately the car didn't survive a major crash, but thankfully Marriott had sustained no lasting injuries. MPL

something monstrous to dethrone the Rocket. In fact, so daunting was the prospect of taking on the American freak that no foreign challengers made the trip to Florida in 1907 leaving the Stanley brothers and Marriott to have a crack at beating their own mark. Unbelievably, a new and improved boiler looked like it might be the catalyst to help them do just that. Despite two deep gullies running across the Daytona course, Marriott managed a 29-second mile in practice. Lining up some nine miles away from the start, he gradually increased the pace towards what has been estimated at anything between 132mph and 200mph. Whatever the true number, when he hit one of the gullies the results were catastrophic.

The car lifted close to 20 feet in the air, before smashing back into the beach some 100 feet further on, having turned sideways while in flight. Rocket was in pieces, with debris scattered far and wide across the beach, and officials feared the worst for the driver.

To great surprise he was, thankfully, alive – albeit unconscious – and with four cracked ribs, a broken breastbone, facial injuries and his right eye hanging out the socket. By coincidence, a doctor was on holiday nearby and had witnessed the incident. He took Marriott to a hotel, ensuring there were no life-threatening injuries before pressing his eye back into place using a spoon. All in a day's work for a land speed record driver.

Marriott retired, recovered and lived to 83, but Rocket was no more. The Stanley special might have been gone, but it would never be forgotten – and it would be nearly four years before internal combustion managed to overhaul its astonishing effort.

Difficult economic circumstances in Europe meant the major names were reluctant to dedicate the required resources to building the type of custom creation that had become a prerequisite of land speed record attempts. For a short time it seemed as if Marriott's mark would last forever, but then from nowhere the oldest name in the business produced a powerhouse.

The new challenger came from Benz, its engine comprising four cylinders in two blocks of two, each with a bore and stroke of 185mm x 200mm meaning capacity was 21.5 litres. Maximum output came at 1600rpm and, while there was nothing particularly remarkable about the car's functional design, some subtle additions and subtractions gave it a wheelbase of just 112 inches and dry weight of around 1350kg. It might have been heavier than some that had come before it, but it had the velocity to do some serious damage.

Like many of the German company's models, its clean lines and perfect proportion made it beautiful to behold. Called the Blitzen (Lightning) Benz, its name was as stunning as its looks – and its early performances lived up to the billing.

After victorious sprint campaigns in Belgium, the Benz was sent to Britain in 1909 along with the team's number-one driver Victor Hémery. The two-year-old race track Brooklands was chosen as the place where the car would make its assault on the land speed record.

Flying kilometre complete, driver and manufacturer waiting anxiously for the confirmed numbers to come through – the news was exactly what they wanted. Hémery had swept

The shimmering white Blitzen Benz was undoubtedly the fastest car in the world from around 1908, and it was proved as such in America and Europe alike. MPL

round the circuit at 125.95mph, duly ratified as a land speed record by the Association International des Automobile Clubs Reconnus (AIACR) the successors of the ACF and new self-appointed ruling body for world motor racing and record attempts.

The French driver went on to try and defeat Marriott's mile time, but on a circular racing circuit rather than a long, straight stretch he was unable to generate sufficient speed. Were someone to take it out on such a course, however, it felt as if the big white Benz was capable of more.

A year later in 1910, the Benz was back, only this time it was in the hands of legendary American racer Barney Oldfield, who'd picked it up for a reported $10,000 from the company's US showroom.

Once in his possession, he wasted little time in unleashing its power on the friendly surface at Daytona, where he blitzed the Blitzen to a mile speed of 131.28mph to finally dethrone Marriott and the Stanley.

Of course, the AIACR was no more accommodating than its predecessor and refused to recognise anything but a flying kilometre as an outright land speed record. Oldfield, like other

Americans before him, dismissed the opinion of the French and anointed himself as 'Holder of the World's Speed Record' – a title he painted on a train he owned.

Largely due to the lobbying of Britain's Royal Automobile Club, later in 1910 the AIACR introduced a new rule stating that from the beginning of the new year any attempt on the world's top speed would need to be made by completing two runs, which would be made across a measured kilometre and also across a measured mile.

The update to the rules, designed to accommodate British and American drivers' use of the 'mph' measurement rather than the European 'kph', stated that both the timed kilometre and timed mile would be measured on the same run. There would be one run in each direction at the same course, to produce two averages – one in kph and one in mph – with the higher being accepted as the record.

If anything, America's 'to hell with Europe' attitude was only strengthened by the new regulations. When Oldfield had his racing permit revoked he sold his prized Benz to another barnstorming Yankee – 'Wild' Bob Burman. After a season of grass- and dirt-track racing, Burman headed for Daytona to test his mettle.

LEFT: Hémery was back on the LSR scene, as top driver for German company Benz. He lines up here (left) with teammates at the US GP of 1911. MPL

LEFT: There was little doubt that the Benz was the fastest car on the planet (whether in the US or Europe), and Oldfield proved it so at Daytona in 1910. MPL

BELOW: The banked course at Brooklands could not tame the Blitzen as Hornsted took it to a new outright best, albeit slower than the existing mark and only designated as a land speed record owing to the increasingly complex rules and regulations laid down by the AIACR. MPL

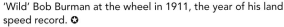

'Wild' Bob Burman at the wheel in 1911, the year of his land speed record. ✪

It was April 1911 by this point, and the new two-way competition was in operation. Clearly that didn't bother 'Wild' Bob as he made a mile-long single run at a claimed speed of 141.37mph – a staggering 10mph faster than Oldfield. The Americans declared it official, the French rejected it out of hand.

When Burman later visited Europe he was asked how he'd managed to extract such pace from the race-weary Benz. His supposed reply? "Nothing to it. We just marked out a mile on the beach before high tide, and when the sea went down again… boy, that mile had shrunk."

Unofficial runs, sceptical claims and a floundering authority – once again the land speed record was somewhat messy. One group that didn't care however was Benz; whether Hémery, Oldfield or Burman (and Benz itself was reluctant to acknowledge the latter) the company had an iron grip on the land speed record. It now just needed to set a two-way mark to complete the full package, and British driver Lydston Hornsted duly obliged.

At Brooklands on June 24, 1914, he made the first run under the AIACR's new two-way format. Hornsted's speed for the first mile was 128.16mph, followed by 120.23mph for the second – certainly proving how favourable wind direction could influence events. His average was 124.10mph, not faster than Hémery's official land speed record but adjudged to have surpassed it nonetheless.

The history books had been rewritten, and a new benchmark speed set. It must have been a fascinating back-and-forth to follow, if perhaps all just a little bit confusing.

Hornsted's Benz was a dark blue 200hp model with a Blitzen-type engine. MPL

Kenelm Lee **Guinness**
A spark of genius

ABOVE:
A triumphant Guinness sits proudly in his
Sunbeam 350 at Brooklands. MPL

▌▌ RECORDS

Date	Speed	Place	Car
May 17, 1922	133.75mph	Brooklands, Great Britain	**Sunbeam 350**

L ike many of his contemporaries, Irish-born, London-based Kenelm Lee Guinness was a motor racing driver who had commercial interests in engineering. In fact, as a member of the Guinness brewing dynasty, one might say that entrepreneurship was in his blood, and he proved as such when he purchased space in a disused pub and began manufacturing his own KLG spark plug.

His own racing experiences had prompted him to produce a more reliable unit, and through innovative use of raw materials he was able to achieve his aim and his product developed a national reputation for stable performance. The KLG brand was in high demand during the First World War for use in aircraft, and as such Guinness was asked to resign from naval duties and remain at home in his factory.

The adrenaline of racing continued to be a lure, however, and in the early 1920s he once again got behind the wheel in competitive action. As well as taking part in and winning several of Europe's major events, he took his Sunbeam team to land speed record glory when he broke Hornsted's eight-year-old mark. He did it in style, too, adding nearly 10mph by posting a run of 133.75mph.

Unfortunately the comeback was not to last, and in 1924 Guinness suffered a horror crash at San Sebastián in Spain during which his riding mechanic was killed. Suffering severe physical injuries, it's possible that he would never have raced again anyway, but the mental trauma he experienced made sure of it. Sadly, it was an episode from which he would ultimately never recover, and 13 years later he was found dead in his bedroom, having apparently committed suicide.

While the end of Guinness's life was certainly tragic, his legacy most definitely lives on with the KLG spark plug still a leading product today. After his retirement, he also sold his record-breaking car to another Sunbeam driver by the name of Malcolm Campbell who gave it the nickname Blue Bird.

RECORDS

Date	Speed	Place	Car
July 6, 1924	143.31mph	Arpajon, France	**Delage**

René **Thomas**   **Flying high**

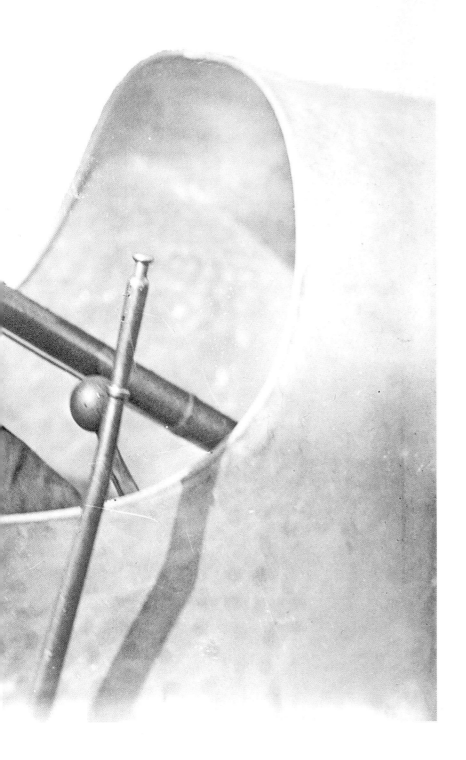

In the years between Hornsted's and Guinness's respective records, two unsanctioned runs in America had yielded speeds of 149mph and 156mph. As impressive as the official land speed record had become, it was apparent that modern vehicles were capable of more than the current mark and Frenchman René Thomas was next to prove it.

One of his country's most talented drivers, his most notable racing achievement was to win the famous Indianapolis 500 event in 1914 – his first of four appearances at the American showpiece. He was also a noted aviator, and reportedly held the somewhat dubious honour of being involved in the world's first mid-air collision in 1910.

It was on the ground where Thomas was at his best, however, and after more than a decade of competitive success he took a car from his Delage team and lifted the LSR up to 143.31mph.

Despite being nearly 10mph better than Guinness's speed, it would take just six days for the new target to be broken once more.

LEFT:
Pioneering pilot and racing revelation, Thomas is pictured during his victorious Indianapolis 500 campaign in 1914. A decade later, he would become the 15th man to officially break the land speed record. Library of Congress ✪

Ernest **Eldridge**
The gambler

	RECORDS			
Date	*Speed*	*Place*		*Car*
July 12, 1924	146.01mph	Arpajon, France		**Fiat Mephistopheles**

A man who became obsessed with cramming huge engines into the smallest of cars, Ernest Eldridge will surely go down as one of the most colourful characters ever associated with the land speed record.

After serving as an ambulance driver and artillery gunner in the First World War, he trained as an engineer. A common theme in the pioneering days of motorsport, the engineer soon became a skilled driver. But unlike many of those who had gone before him, Eldridge's passion for speed far outweighed his love of road racing.

His first notable creation was a small Italian Isotta-Fraschini that the Briton fitted with a monstrous 20-litre Maybach aircraft engine. To the consternation of spectators, Eldridge took the unique machine around the famous Brooklands circuit at more than 100mph.

The 240hp beast was sold in order to purchase a 10-litre Fiat, the second car then used to dismantle a series of speed records across Europe. Eldridge's winnings bought him a second Fiat christened Mephistopheles, named after a demon from German folklore, and after breaking the record for the half-mile from a standing start he set his sights on LSR history.

In July 1924, less than a week after Thomas had recorded his own world best, Eldridge blasted Mephistopheles to 146.01mph and captured the ultimate speed prize.

Goal achieved, he turned his attention to a grand prix career and endurance races. During a campaign in the latter, his front axle collapsed, causing his car to somersault. Eldridge suffered serious head injuries as well as losing an eye.

A man with a famed love of gambling (he once lost £60,000 on the turn of one card in a Monte Carlo casino) had finally lost, and the extent of the damage resulted in retirement.

Speed was never far from Eldridge's mind though, and he became mentor and manager to Captain George Eyston – a student who would become a master.

Aged 40, returning from a trip to Bonneville, Eldridge contracted and sadly succumbed to pneumonia, and with his passing the world lost an unforgettable figure of motorsport.

LEFT:
The eccentric Eldridge sits in what was probably his greatest creation and the vehicle in which he broke the land speed record – the mammoth 21.7-litre Fiat Mephistopheles. MPL

CHAPTER FIVE

133.75MPH ➡ 146.01MPH

The American Ralph de Palma showcases the V12 Packard at Daytona in 1919. MPL

SETTING THE RECORD STRAIGHT

As with nearly all aspects of life, the First World War halted interest in and pursuit of the land speed record. Among the millions of casualties claimed in the great conflict of 1914-1918 were a number of the famous racers of the time (and plenty of lesser-known competitors, too), and many of those who were fortunate enough to return home did so with career-ending injuries. But return they did, and slowly but surely normal life was resumed.

Within a couple of years, attention had turned back to motor sport – and a younger generation wanting distractions to help them forget the horrors faced in the trenches of western Europe had become ardent followers.

When it came to record-breaking, it would have been better for the new legion of fans – and the existing ones, for that matter – if the record was a nice, neat linear progression. Unfortunately no such thing existed, and continued American attempts meant the confusion would go on for a number of years yet.

Noted racing champion Ralph de Palma was first to reignite the pursuit of speed supremacy. Horsted's two-way average of 124.10mph around Brooklands might have been recognised by the governing bodies as the official land speed record, but de Palma was out to prove the Benz was no longer the world's fastest car – and on February 12, 1919, at Daytona, he did exactly that.

By this time, the US authorities and US competitors were well aware of the AIACR's regulations, so it seemed strange that de Palma made only one pass through the flying mile in his V12 Packard when a second pass may well have given him an official speed. As it was, he completed that mile in a rip-roaring 24.02 seconds at 149.88mph – but still not eligible to enter the record books.

As had been the case before the war, the US was happy to accept this new effort as 'the record'. De Palma was equally dismissive of European jurisdiction and claimed to be the world's fastest; that was until his countryman Tommy Milton took a twin-engine Duesenberg to a shattering 156.03mph through the mile at Daytona in 1920. Reports and recollections over the subsequent course of events differ – some suggest Milton continued on in an effort to break longer-distance records, the man himself claiming he made a return run. Whatever the truth, after the first mile his car ignited and at the end of the course he had to put the blaze out himself using the Florida sand.

The doubts over the legitimacy of the run, probably combined with its own disposition towards the rebellious Americans, meant the AIACR once again rejected any notion of this being a new land speed record. Hornsted retained the official title at what had become a rather embarrassing 30mph slower.

Tommy Milton was one in a long line of unofficial American record-breakers, claiming the 'crown' in 1920. Here he is in the Duesenberg. MPL

A RAY OF LIGHT FROM SUNBEAM

Like every great narrative, the land speed record was in desperate need of a hero. It had become a messy web of sub-plots and side issues that took away from the incredible bravery and ingenious engineering of those aiming to push the boundaries of how fast man and car could travel across the earth. At the start of the 1920s a hero did indeed arrive, and it was a 350hp stunner from the Sunbeam factory in the British city of Wolverhampton.

Unlike its successors, this first incarnation of the record-breaking Sunbeam was a versatile contender that had demonstrated capabilities in track events and hill climbing before it was unleashed on the speed record scene. This particular challenger was also the first aero-engine LSR car, and it gave rise to a new era of developing aviation technology being deployed in such vehicles.

Those vehicles were getting slightly heavier, too – the Sunbeam weighing in at a little more than 1600kg. But power was increasing at a far greater rate, with a massive 18.3-litre V12 unit providing significant impetus.

When the team put its new car in the hands of Kenelm Lee Guinness at Brooklands on May 17, 1922, every precaution was taken to prevent French obstruction. Sunbeam saw to it that the timing equipment used was officially and explicitly approved by the AIACR, and it was arranged that a sealed envelope with the day's results would be sent to the authority's Paris headquarters for verification.

The concrete at the famous Weybridge circuit was not helpful for speed runs given its banked nature, but nevertheless a course was set up along the flat Railway Straight between the Members' and Byfleet corners.

Guinness used the full outer circuit to reach top speed, or as close to it as he could given the curves, and as he swept through the marked stretch he posted 130.5mph for the flying kilometre into the wind and an impressive 137.15mph with its assistance. The final result was 133.75mph, and Hornsted's record had at last been officially broken.

KLG's mark lasted for two years, his one and only moment of LSR glory. It was also the final time the record was captured at Brooklands, but it was by no means the last victory for Sunbeam.

The team's cars would break the outright best a further four times, and would form a legendary partnership with a certain Malcolm Campbell. However, before that, there was a dramatic tussle set to unfold across the English Channel.

LEFT: The 350 was the first in an impressive series of speed specials from Sunbeam, and here Guinness prepares the model for his glorious run at Brooklands in 1922. MPL

Before Campbell went on to his unrivalled decade of dominance, Frenchman René Thomas and his English rival Ernest Eldridge would go head to head for Guinness's and Sunbeam's crown – the duel offering nostalgic resemblance to the famous struggle between Chasseloup-Laubat and Jenatzy a quarter-century before.

Thomas had at his command a Delage, a machine from his home country that had appeared on the scene in 1923 in a hill climb outside Paris and showed genuine potential as a record-breaker.

France, the spiritual home of the LSR, had not produced the world's fastest vehicle since 1905 and so excitement grew when the driver took the big V12 to the Geneva Speed Trials

and clocked 129.30mph for a one-way kilometre. Realising something special might be in the offing, the Moto Club de France (MCF) decided to host a records meeting at Arpajon on July 6 the following year.

Thomas and theDelage were soon entered, as was Eldridge and his Fiat – an immense creation housing a six-cylinder, 24-valve, 300hp A-12 aviation engine that provided a daunting 21,714cc. It was christened Mephistopheles, a German demon from a tale by Faust, but the name was clearly given on account of its abilities and not its looks because it had a brutal attractiveness and epitomised the cutting edge of 1920s high-speed car design.

A variety of three- and four-wheeled

categories were run before the main 'over five-litre' event featuring just Thomas and Eldridge. It was the Frenchman who had the honours, and the mighty Delage produced a smooth yet incredibly swift average run of 143.31mph for the kilometre and 143.26mph for the mile on the dangerously narrow stretch of countryside road.

The Sunbeam had been toppled, and Thomas had won a great victory for his country – if only for a few minutes.

Unlike the Delage, Mephistopheles was anything but smooth and it burst off the line with a bestial roar, wheels spinning before it gathered pace and began swinging side to side to strike fear into the crowds lined

LEFT: Sunbeam meant business in all manner of motoring events from sprints and hill climbs to the prestigious Grand Prix of the day. Its line-up at the 1922 French GP was highly impressive, comprising Jean Chassagne, Guinness and Henry Segrave. ○

RIGHT: René Thomas and the Delage made an impact in the years after the First World War, and the car became the first French production to capture the land speed record for nearly 15 years – although it was only able to hold on to the title for a mere six days. ○

In one of the most popular record-breaking runs in the history of the competition, Eldridge captured the land speed record in the odd-looking and undoubtedly fast Mephistopheles less than a week after being controversially beaten by Thomas at Arpajon. MPL

up alarmingly close to the route. As Eldridge blasted back across following his second run, the results came in; 146.80mph for the kilometre and 145.20mph for the mile. The day had its second land speed record holder, or so it seemed.

It remains unclear whether he made the decision alone or was encouraged to do so by passionate compatriots who were determined to keep the crown, but Thomas almost immediately lodged a complaint on the grounds Mephistopheles had no reverse gear – a requirement that had been drafted with the intention of keeping LSR vehicles within the bounds of normal automotive design. The organisers were left with little option; Eldridge was disqualified and it was Thomas who departed Arpajon the victor.

Eldridge vowed to right the wrong immediately, and spent a solid 48 hours at his hired Paris workshop installing a reverse gear on the vast Fiat.

Six days later he was generously granted a rerun and, at first light, the car – compliance with the rules confirmed – coughed and spluttered away from the line. The best average was 142.38mph for the mile, but Eldridge was not surprised to hear he'd fallen short – this was just the warm-up.

Carburation slightly adjusted and burst tyre replaced, he bounded back across the course and exacted crushing revenge on the 'unsporting' Thomas with an average for the kilometre of 146.01mph and a stunning new land speed record. Despite the fact an Englishman had beaten their

man on home soil in a special of Italian descent, the French crowd were overjoyed and praised Eldridge for his determination to come back from cruel defeat.

Even though the new time was still a little short of Milton's, because it was an average of two runs there wasn't really an argument to be made that the Fiat wasn't the fastest car in the world. For the first time in a long time it seemed as if there was one undisputed record – Mephistopheles and Eldridge held it, but Campbell was waiting in the wings to win it back for Sunbeam.

Sir Malcolm **Campbell**
Land speed legend

ABOVE:
Campbell, in white sweatshirt and trademark goggles, poses with a crowd next to his Sunbeam 350 during a racing event in Skegness, Great Britain. MPL

A hero of what was a golden age for land speed exploits, Sir Malcolm Campbell stands out as perhaps the greatest record-breaker of all time.

He was born in 1885 as the only son of a British diamond trader and initially went into the family business. A fascination with motor racing, particularly on two wheels, soon developed and when he returned to London in the early 20th century he focused his time and efforts on his new passion.

He found early success, too, but the outbreak of the First World War interrupted his blossoming career. Enlisting as a motorcycle dispatch rider, Campbell soon saw action and fought in the Battle of Mons in 1914; he was later drafted into the Royal Flying Corps where he served as a pilot.

A relative latecomer to speed trials, it was after the conflict had ended that he turned his attention to breaking records on both land and water. He returned to Brooklands, where he'd raced before his military service, and acquired Guinness's Sunbeam – a car that had been taken to a land speed record of 133.75mph. Making a series of modifications, Campbell twice achieved better efforts only to be denied official recognition due to the nature of the timing equipment used to measure his runs. Finally, in 1924, his dream was achieved as he bettered Eldridge's new mark by less than a quarter of a mile per hour. It would prove to be just the beginning of an 11-year affinity with the historic competition. By the time Campbell made history for the final time in 1935, becoming the first man to surpass 300mph in the process, he was a nine-time holder of the land speed record and had cemented his status as an all-time legend of the game. He was also knighted for his efforts, becoming Sir Malcolm Campbell in 1931. Not content, he later turned his attention to the water speed record and reclaimed the title for Great Britain in 1937 when he took Blue Bird K3 to 126.33mph on Lake Maggiore on the Italian-Swiss border. He further extended the mark by reaching 141.74mph on Coniston Water in England's Lake District – a record that stood for 11 years.

With Campbell still an active member of the British military, the onset of the Second World War put paid to any further history-making attempts. During the late 1930s he commanded a division of the Territorial Army, and between 1940 and 1942 he was at the head of a military police contingent that was tasked with evacuating King George VI, his consort Queen Elizabeth and their daughters out of London in the event of an invasion by Nazi Germany. At a time when so many speed record-seekers lost their lives in accidents and crashes, Campbell was one of the few to die of natural causes – succumbing to a series of strokes in 1948 aged 63. Given his success in different vehicles and on a variety of surfaces, Campbell had achieved fame internationally and news of his death was met with tributes around the world.

RECORDS

Date	Speed	Place	Car
September 25, 1924	146.16mph	Pendine Sands, Great Britain	**Sunbeam**
July 21, 1925	150.87mph	Pendine Sands, Great Britain	**Blue Bird**
February 4, 1927	174.88mph	Pendine Sands, Great Britain	**Blue Bird**
February 19, 1928	206.96mph	Daytona Beach, USA	**Blue Bird**
February 5, 1931	246.09mph	Daytona Beach, USA	**Blue Bird**
February 24, 1932	253.97mph	Daytona Beach, USA	**Blue Bird**
February 22, 1933	272.46mph	Daytona Beach, USA	**Blue Bird**
March 7, 1935	276.82mph	Daytona Beach, USA	**Blue Bird**
September 3, 1935	301.13mph	Bonneville Salt Flats, USA	**Blue Bird**

Sir Henry **Segrave**
The 200mph man

RECORDS			
Date	*Speed*	*Place*	*Car*
March 21, 1926	152.33mph	Southport, Great Britain	**Sunbeam Tiger**
March 29, 1927	203.79mph	Daytona Beach, USA	**Sunbeam Mystery**
March 11, 1929	231.45mph	Daytona Beach, USA	**Golden Arrow**

Although he was more than 10 years younger, the life of Sir Henry Segrave followed a similar pattern to that of Campbell – a man with whom he would form an intense rivalry.

Born in Baltimore, USA, to an American mother and Irish father, Segrave moved to the UK at a young age and assumed his British nationality. While he was too young to compete in the years preceding the First World War, he had developed a strong interest in motor racing before being called up to serve as an infantryman and fighter pilot. Such were his talents that he was recruited to the Royal Air Force in 1919, but resigned due to the effects of injuries sustained in the conflict.

His ailments could not stop him racing, however, and after lobbying team bosses for a chance to demonstrate his ability at Brooklands he was eventually given a ride. He responded with victory, and that was followed by wins in the French GP and at San Sebastian – both achieved in a Sunbeam – which made him the first British driver to win a grand prix in a British-made car.

From his days as a pilot Segrave had always had a fascination with speed, and he had boasted to anyone who would listen that he'd one day drive a car at 200mph. With racing success in the bank, he turned his attention to making that claim a reality. Segrave's first effort in 1926 saw him take the land speed record from Campbell, as the coveted mark passed 150mph for the first time. The latter responded in style and had lifted the top speed to 174.88mph by 1927, but Segrave had bigger ambitions in mind.

With it now possible to set official records in the USA, he took his 1000hp Sunbeam to Daytona – a venue that had yielded significant speeds in the past – and he proved true to his word by obliterating all that had gone before to earn a new land speed record of 203.79mph. He was not finished there either, and returned to the Florida beach with Golden Arrow in 1929, setting a speed of 231.45mph – an effort it would take Campbell two years to improve.

With his lofty aims realised, Segrave set his sights on his other great passion – boat racing. From Daytona he headed straight south down the American east coast to Miami where he inflicted an embarrassing defeat on national hero Garfield Wood, a competitor who'd not lost a race in nine years.

Having beaten his rival, he vowed to wrestle the water land speed record from the American's grasp and returned to England where he built a seven-tonne, 4000hp craft he christened Miss England II. Segrave launched the boat on to Lake Windermere on June 13, 1930, just two months after he'd received a knighthood, and promptly recorded 96.41mph through the mile, then 101.11mph in the return leg.

A new record had been set, but because of the time needed to corroborate the results it could not be immediately confirmed – and Segrave felt he could go faster still. During the third run, Miss England II capsized, knocking its pilot unconscious. Segrave came round briefly in hospital to be told that he'd indeed broken the water speed record and become the first man to hold both the water and land titles simultaneously. Sadly though, his injuries were too great and he died shortly after due to the damage sustained by his lungs.

To mark his incredible achievements, the Segrave Trophy was named in his honour and is still presented annually to the person from Britain or the Commonwealth who is deemed to have accomplished the greatest achievement in the air, on land or on water. Past recipients include Amy Johnson, Geoff Duke, Stirling Moss, Richard Branson, Joey Dunlop, John Surtees and Lewis Hamilton.

Malcolm Campbell was awarded the honour in 1933 and 1939.

LEFT:
At the Sunbeam factory, Segrave sits aboard the famed Sunbeam 1000 in which he achieved the first ever land speed record to exceed 200mph. MPL

John Parry-Thomas

An unexpected Welsh hero

ABOVE:
Parry-Thomas, in the centre wearing goggles,
stands with Babs on Pendine Sands. MPL

RECORDS			
Date	Speed	Place	Car
April 27, 1926	169.30mph	Pendine Sands, Great Britain	**Higham Special Babs**
April 28, 1926	171.02mph	Pendine Sands, Great Britain	**Higham Special Babs**

Anative of Wales, John Parry-Thomas spectacularly entered the land speed picture at a time when it seemed Campbell and Seagrave had established an iron grip on the record.

Born in 1884, he had studied engineering at college in London before the First World War and after serving his time in the military he became chief engineer for Leyland Motors. Along with Reid Railton he had helped bring the luxury Leyland Eight vehicle to market and as a keen driver, Parry-Thomas took his creation on to the track at Brooklands where he won a total of 38 races in five seasons.

Such was his success that he decided to try his hand at record breaking, driven in part by the idea that capturing some of the notable titles of the day would bring his employers greater recognition around the world. He purchased a suitable vehicle from the estate of Count Louis Zborowski – the racer having been killed at the Italian GP – and began work on modifications to bring the Higham Special up to the standard required to take on the fastest cars around.

Parry-Thomas embarked on several test runs in 1925, but his inferior 27-litre Liberty V12 aero engine couldn't compete with the powerplants Campbell and Segrave had at their disposals – and the Welshman didn't have the financial backing or factory team finances to afford an upgrade.

Still, he knew he could at least get close and so took the car on to Pendine Sands in 1926 for an official attempt. To widespread consternation he not only eclipsed Segrave's speed, but raised the land speed record from 152.33mph to 169.30mph. Encountering poor weather conditions and soft sand on a second run the following day, the new record-holder somehow managed to go even faster and elevated the target to a fraction more than 171mph.

Campbell, who had already resolved to claim back the crown from Segrave, immediately got to work on preparing Blue Bird – but Parry-Thomas had already proved he was no pushover and continued modifying his own mount. He returned to the seven-mile stretch of sand in his home country a year later, no longer in ownership of the land speed record but determined to be the first man to break the three-miles-a-minute barrier.

Now with the considerable support of both Shell and Dunlop, a confident Parry-Thomas took Babs – the new name of his car – through a routine warm-up before lining up on the course. During the first timed run his rear suspension collapsed, causing a major accident. The driver was pronounced dead at the scene, having been partially decapitated, and he was subsequently buried near the track at Brooklands where he'd made his name. Such were the perils of racing at the time, particularly in speed runs, that such horrific incidents were sadly quite commonplace.

Parry-Thomas's team of engineers, including Reid Railton, went on to work for Campbell and were instrumental in the development of the Blue Bird vehicles used to conquer the land speed record multiple times in the 1930s.

Charles **Raymond Keech**

An American makes his mark

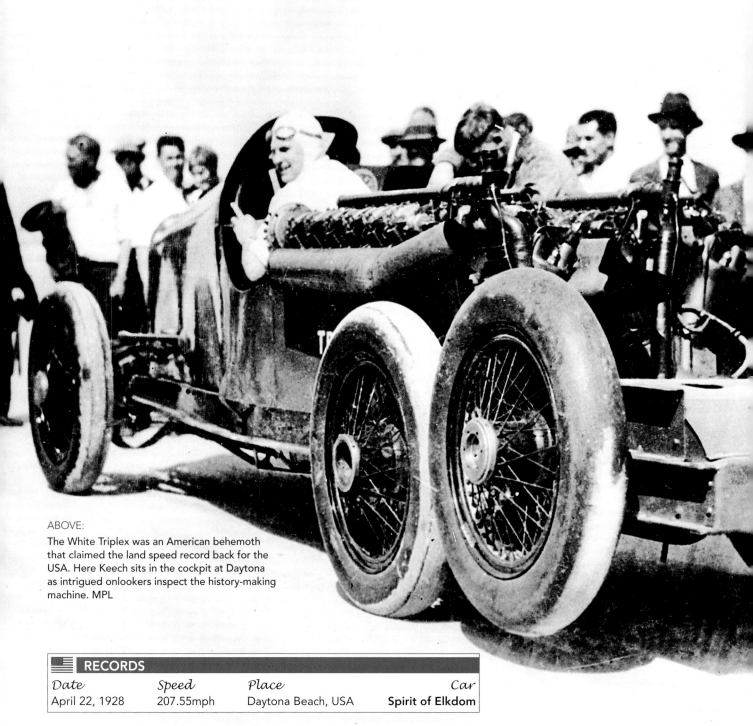

ABOVE:
The White Triplex was an American behemoth
that claimed the land speed record back for the
USA. Here Keech sits in the cockpit at Daytona
as intrigued onlookers inspect the history-making
machine. MPL

	RECORDS			
Date	*Speed*	*Place*		*Car*
April 22, 1928	207.55mph	Daytona Beach, USA		**Spirit of Elkdom**

Charles Raymond Keech, known commonly as Ray, arrived into a farming family in rural Pennsylvania, USA, in 1900 – the first land speed record holder born in the 20th century.

Despite spending his formative years helping to deliver milk to the local markets, joining the business was never a likely long-term plan and he was soon making the most of his spare time by working on cars and trucks.

Employed by the local mechanic, Keech earned a reputation for truck racing before he transitioned to the popular American endeavour of dirt track, where he took several victories and earned multiple records.

Pursuing a lucrative motor racing career, he moved his family to Philadelphia in 1927 where he was scouted by wealthy manufacturer Jim White. Not since Vanderbilt in 1902 had the USA held the land speed record, and it'd been the best part of a decade before an American had even laid claim to an unofficial top speed. White wanted to change that, and enlisted Keech to build and pilot a machine capable of doing the job.

Showing how serious they were, the duo relocated the team to Daytona Beach a year later where they unleashed their new triple-engine, 36-cylinder, 81-litre monster creation. However, on the first run Keech was scalded by boiling water from a split hose, and then he had to contend with an engine fire during his second attempt. To add insult to injury, a timing malfunction meant the speed couldn't be verified – and those who witnessed it knew it was quick.

With no complaints, Keech simply returned to the vehicle and promptly completed another run, during which he clocked 207.55mph. The land speed record belonged to an American once more.

His standing had never been higher, but such was the difficulty he'd encountered he declared that he'd never use the car for a speed trial again. When mechanic Lee Bible was killed behind its wheel attempting to reclaim the land speed crown for White later in the decade, Keech concluded that record-breaking was too dangerous and turned his attention to winning what he saw as the world's most prestigious motoring event – the Indianapolis 500.

Demonstrating his considerable talent, Keech claimed victory in the race in 1929; and he did so in emphatic style by averaging just short of 100mph and finishing an astonishing six minutes ahead of his nearest rival.

Having quit record attempts owing to the danger, it was cruel irony that just two weeks after his exploits at the hallowed Brickyard he was killed at the notorious Altoona Speedway. Having come away from an initial accident unscathed, he was hit by another car as he attempted to crawl off the track and was unable to recover from the injuries sustained.

A MAN NAMED CAMPBELL

Malcolm Campbell,
perhaps the most
famous record-breaker
of them all. MPL

Malcolm Campbell had witnessed what Sunbeam could do when Guinness captured the land speed record in 1922, and from that moment the Englishman developed a long-lasting love affair with the competition – a love affair leading to greatness. He'd already proved his skills as a racer at Brooklands before the First World War, and that helped him convince team chief Louis Coatalen to allow the big 350hp out for a blast on the sands at Saltburn in North Yorkshire. No official timekeeping had been organised, but Campbell showed just a glimpse of what was to come as he recorded a one-way run of 134mph on the stopwatch – a speed that put him very much in the mix with the world's fastest.

Determined to turn his early form into long-term success, Campbell set about purchasing the car from Sunbeam – Coatalen initially resistant to his overtures. Realising that perhaps more powerful vehicles were in the team's future, the boss of the Wolverhampton outfit eventually succumbed and in 1923 Campbell got what he desired; although not without having to part with an unspecified but large sum of money. His new purchase was immediately entered into speed trials at Fanoe, a holiday island off the coast of Denmark.

In a stunning run on soft sand, the Sunbeam was taken to an average speed of 137.72mph for the mile – some 4mph faster than Guinness's existing record. Campbell was naturally delighted and it seemed the newcomer had capped his first year of speed events with the ultimate prize; but unfortunately for him the winning feeling was to be short-lived. Unbeknownst to Campbell, the electrical timing system used by the Danes was not the type approved by the governing AIACR. The Paris-based authority even confirmed the accuracy of the recorded speeds, but flatly refused to recognise it as a new outright best. Once again, controversy had reared its head in the world's premier test of automotive speed.

Disappointed but not deterred, Campbell set about several modifications to the 350 Sunbeam in a bid to extract even more from its tremendous powerplant. During the first half of 1924 the works were carried out in London – a longer tail with head fairing was added along with a covered-in rear suspension and radiator cowling. When the car reappeared later in the year it did so in Campbell's favourite colour, and was named Blue Bird.

ABOVE: Campbell always looked at ease in the 350 Sunbeam. MPL

Adjustments are made to the Sunbeam at Pendine. MPL

SUCCESS AT LAST

He once again entered the Fanoe event but by the time it arrived in August, Thomas and then Eldridge had completed their storied duel at Arpajon and Campbell was now faced with 146.01mph rather than 133.75mph that had been the target a year prior. The beach was in even worse condition than had been encountered before, too, and Campbell also warned organisers that crowds were too close to the course. To cause even further concern, during its first run through the mile-long stretch Blue Bird skidded and shed both its rear tyres.

Campbell and his mechanic Leo Villa made changes to the affected wheels as they took most of the car's thrust; the front pair were left as they were. As driver and car embarked on the official record attempt, the

left-hand front tyre flew off as Blue Bird reached up to 150mph. Campbell managed to achieve a controlled stop, but the tyre hit a child among the spectators before ripping through the timing hut – eventually ending up in the sea.

The meeting was halted and, tragically, the young boy died as a result of his injuries in hospital. Fanoe's beach was never again used for LSR activity, and Campbell returned home shaken by the horrific incident and still without the title he so desperately craved.

A month later he was back in pursuit, and this time had found a beach a little closer to home in South Wales – it was known as Pendine Sands.

At seven miles long it provided a

perfect venue for record breaking, but as Blue Bird was prepared for yet another assault it looked as if weather may intervene once more. Boggy patches of sand meant Campbell was restricted to 145.24mph on his first run but, while many a contender would have retired and returned in friendlier conditions, the Englishman hit the sand the following day determined to finally achieve his dream.

This time the wind was even stronger, but he produced a two-way average for the kilometre of 146.16mph to claim a new world best by a whisker.

For a short time he rejoiced, but soon his insatiable appetite for making history came to the fore once again and he set his sights on reaching 150mph – a significant milestone now

just 4mph away. Campbell was sure Blue Bird was capable of such a speed, but with ambitious plans to build a new car he put the legendary Sunbeam up for sale. It was listed at £1500, 'capable of breaking its own record in better weather'. Despite this, and the chance to own a genuine record-breaker, there were no takers.

For the start of 1925, the AIACR had introduced new rules for land speed records. There were no significant changes to format, but it solidified the existing set of guidelines and served to cement the prestige of the 'official' record that was now the dominant mark in the scene.

It also generated renewed interest from manufacturers, who were once again making forays into record-breaking to boost reputations in the commercial market now the financial restrictions of the First World War were finally subsiding.

With rumours of capable vehicles being produced across Europe,

Campbell the record-breaker in action. MPL

Campbell decided his own project was too far from completion to risk letting his rivals catch his 'gettable' record. On July 21, 1925, the unsold Blue Bird was wheeled out for one last crack

and Campbell proved his sales pitch true as he eclipsed both his own best and 150mph under the summer sun at Pendine.

SUNBEAM AND SEGRAVE

Campbell's mile speed of 150.87mph was the outright world record, and it was third time the old Sunbeam had captured the title confirming the team's place as the fastest in the world. It was no surprise then that the next successful challenger used the famous marque to launch a campaign.

However it was curious that as pioneers in the use of huge aviation engines for LSR cars, the Sunbeam in question was a small four-litre model that defied accepted wisdom by achieving success in Grand Prix, hill climbs and sprints before moving up to record-breaking. Despite the modest capacity, it was remarkably light (nearly 700kg less than Blue Bird) and its power-to-weight ratio meant a theoretical speed of 160mph. It proved to be a popular contender, too – enthusiasts perhaps excited by its elegant appearance in comparison to the brutish and crude specials that had dominated for years.

Picked to drive this intriguing new creation was Henry Segrave, a winner for Sunbeam in the 1923 French GP and several other road races. Running on only 11 of the 12 cylinders, tests at Brooklands in late 1925 yielded 145mph and so the scene was set for a record attempt the following year.

In March, the team took the little red firecracker to Southport in England for Segrave to show the world what it could do. The car struggled to stay grounded on the bumpy beach, and in its first runs sustained damage to supercharger casings that threatened to end its bid. Segrave managed to convince engineers to give him just three more minutes of life – he was ready for a full run,

and that was all he'd need.

The first pass was completed safely, on little more than three-quarter throttle. Sensing he was within range of Campbell's effort, and knowing the car had more to give, Segrave opened up and approached the end of the second kilometre at top speed when he hit a gully.

Subsequent measuring of tyre tracks showed the gap between where the car leapt into the air and landed back on the sand was a staggering 49 feet, but somehow the Sunbeam crossed the line as intended to post an average of 152.33mph and a new land speed record.

Campbell and Blue Bird had been defeated, and it was a car with an engine a quarter of the size that had dethroned them. It seemed unlikely that the story would end there.

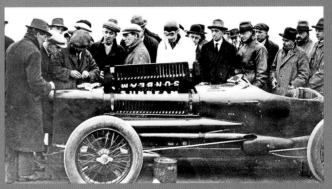

The slight, but super-quick, Sunbeam taken to LSR glory by Segrave. MPL

Parry-Thomas puts Babs through its paces at Brooklands in 1926. MPL

CAMPBELL vs PARRY-THOMAS

As Campbell plotted his response, a new land speed heavyweight entered the fray – his name was John Parry-Thomas. The foreboding Welshman might not have looked much like a racing driver, but he was a genius engineer and the brains behind the highly popular Leyland Eight luxury car.

Throughout 1925 he'd been working his magic to turn a Higham Special purchased from the estate of killed English-born racing driver Count Louis Zborowski into something capable of a genuine LSR attempt. The result was

a modified-for-speed 400hp, 26.9-litre, aero-engine super-monster that was polar opposite to Segrave's nimble Sunbeam.

After an intense period of testing, Parry-Thomas took his newly christened Babs on to the sands at Pendine on April 25, 1926, and it thundered off the line amidst a wave of thick black smoke bellowing from its 12 stub exhausts.

The engine failed to run perfectly throughout either pass, but still Babs smashed Segrave's six-week-old record by just shy of 17mph with an

average kilometre of 169.30mph.

It must have seemed that such a leap would stand for years, but actually it lasted as a land speed record for just 24 hours. Parry-Thomas, not content with the constant misfiring, adjusted the carburation overnight and then went back out again the following day.

Babs was not completely cured, but was certainly in better order – demonstrated by its imposing 171.02mph that left Segrave and Campbell trailing in its wake.

While Sunbeam worked on yet another new record car (believed to be capable of reaching a lofty 200mph), Campbell's built-from-scratch Blue Bird was completed and unveiled in November 1926 – and what a beautiful machine it was. A First World War Napier Lion aircraft engine – 450hp, 22.3-litre – was squeezed into a sleek chassis, painted of course in the owner's favourite shade. It was a simply stunning design, but with every component specially made it was one of the most expensive ever produced. In fact, it's reckoned that Campbell poured nearly £10,000 into the second

LEFT: Rolling out on to the sand at Pendine, Parry-Thomas prepares for a record run. MPL

incarnation of Blue Bird – that compared to the £125 Parry-Thomas spent to purchase Babs, and the £800 he needed to make it LSR ready. With such significant funds invested, Campbell was intent on being first to 180mph – three miles per minute – and he refused to wait in his bid to reach the landmark.

On New Year's Day, 1927, he took the car to Pendine but stalled soon after beginning a run and began sinking into the wet sand. He returned a fortnight later and made several runs, but problems with the gearbox, braking and bodywork meant any considerations of a record attempt were dismissed once again. Finally, a third trip brought success.

Babs gets a wheel change at Pendine. MPL

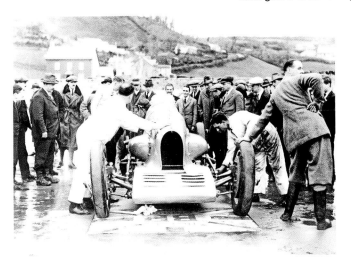

The Sunbeam team prepare the new Blue Bird at Pendine. MPL

Ready to run, Campbell gets set to unleash the Napier Lion engine across the Welsh course. MPL

TRIUMPH AND TRAGEDY

On February 4, 1927, began a memorable two-month period for the land speed record – albeit memorable at times for all the wrong reasons.

First, on that day, Malcolm Campbell and the new Blue Bird roared through the first pass of a record attempt at just short of 180mph – and a speed just over on the return would bring the average he sought. During that return he hit a bump that lifted him into the airstream running over his aerodynamically shaped car, strong enough to whip the goggles from his face. Controlling Blue Bird with one hand as he pulled them back over his eyes, he lost speed and posted only just above 170mph for the second pass.

Yes, the average was 3mph faster than Parry-Thomas and Babs at 174.88mph and it meant Campbell had a trio of land speed records to his name. But it was tinged with disappointment because he knew he'd missed a chance at 180mph and now he had to depart the stage

and let Parry-Thomas and maybe Segrave's new Sunbeam respond.

It was his Welsh rival that had first go, but on Thursday, March 3, came one of the darkest days in LSR history as the pursuit of the world's outright fastest speed resulted in its first driver fatality. No one knows whether John Parry-Thomas had claimed back his record from Campbell; although he had completed his second run the devastating effects of his accident destroyed the timing wire. Whatever the truth, whatever did actually cause Babs to overturn, Britain lost a great driver and a much-loved character.

Then, with the dust barely settled on the tragic events at Pendine, Segrave and Sunbeam emerged at Daytona with their much-vaunted 1000hp Sunbeam on March 29. If rumour was to be believed, the duo was going to launch the land speed record into the mind-boggling realm of 200mph.

200mph at DAYTONA

Sun shining down, a delightfully warm day with a perfect cooling breeze from the sea and 30,000 spectators ready and waiting; on March 29, 1927, the scene was set at Daytona for one of the most glorious moments in the history of the land speed record. It was a scene that had come about when Henry Segrave posed the question to Sunbeam manager Louis Coatalen: what about 200mph?

Malcolm Campbell, Sunbeam's former champion and now its chief rival, was publicly targeting three miles per minute (180mph), so it wasn't unreasonable to expect more. The Segrave-Coatalen combination had shocked the world once already with their small yet efficient four-litre V12, but it'd been an exception rather than the rule – a rule that said the aero engine was king. And so now if power was the prerequisite of record-breaking, then the pair were going to make the most powerful car ever seen.

Campbell had proved the Napier Lion to be the pre-eminent aviation engine of its time, but if Sunbeam were to produce an LSR challenger then it would have to house the company's own engine. Knowing a Sunbeam powerplant couldn't beat what was housed in Blue Bird, Coatalen simply selected two of his 22.5-litre, V12, four-camshaft, 48-valve Matabele engines and then set about deciding how they would fit in one streamlined chassis.

What he came up with mirrored the work of Mors and Stanley before, with the body shaped like an upturned boat – the engines sitting at the front and back, either side of the driver. Jack Irving was handed the task of turning the idea into reality, and it was given the imposing name of 1000hp Sunbeam – although power was in reality a little less.

As the team began building, Segrave turned his attention to arranging a record run. It was calculated the new monster would need a course at least nine miles

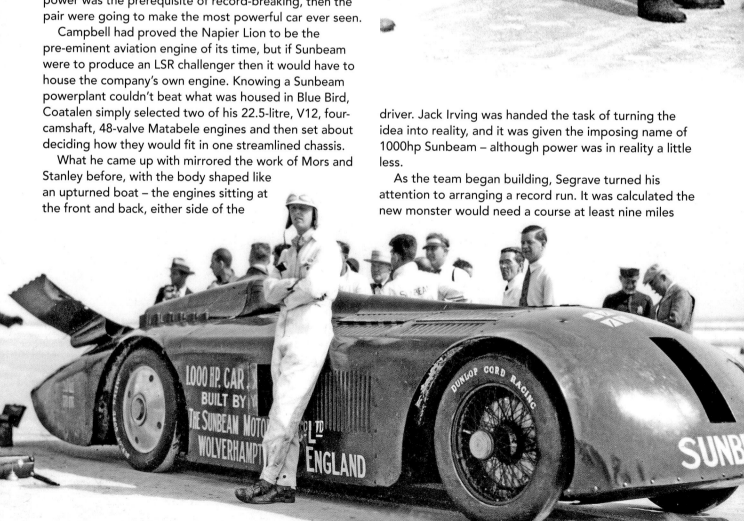

Segrave and the incredible 1000hp Sunbeam at Daytona. MPL

long, and that ruled out any beach in Great Britain or indeed even in Europe.

Segrave's backers were adamant that the attempt should be made on home soil, but the driver was certain that the beach at Daytona – home to so many memorable efforts – was the only venue suitable. Such was his conviction he offered to cover transport at his own expense, and he would personally pay the mechanics that joined the travelling party. One problem solved, he moved on to his next – persuading the American Automobile Association to join the AIACR.

A charm and diplomacy that made him a much-loved figure in the motoring world was enough to do the job, and the US governing body agreed to use the approved electrical timing apparatus and to provide independent certificates of accuracy.

Months of work and effort complete, finally the Sunbeam was ready. Having watched it during testing, Segrave spoke about the 1000hp beast in awe: "I shall never forget my sensations when I first heard its engines running all out. No words can describe the unimaginable output of power which the machinery seemed to catapult into the building. It was one continuous deafening roar, the wheels spinning round like semi-invisible discs at

210mph." The time had come for the great Englishman to put that power into action on the Florida sand but, as if just to tease the fevered crowd, the first run did not go as planned.

Having just about managed to negate the effects of a strong cross-wind, the brakes failed to sufficiently slow the Sunbeam and Segrave had to deliberately steer for the shallow sea in order to come to a halt. Hitting the water at around 55mph the car sent up great jets – the 30,000 were certainly getting a show.

Once again tackling swerves caused by the swirling breeze, Segrave managed to successfully blast through the two required runs – and suddenly the excited spectators fell silent as they waited for the all-important results. The announcement came, and it revealed the flying mile to have produced the highest average speed – a sensational 203.79mph.

Campbell's hard-won record, less than a month old, had been eclipsed by Segrave and Sunbeam. In fact it had been obliterated, the 28mph increase representing the biggest leap in the history of the LSR to date. News of the remarkable feat travelled fast around the world, and the congratulations poured in. Among the messages was a telegram that read: "Damn good show – Campbell."

A stunning view along the beach at Daytona demonstrates the significant following that speed record attempts had accrued by the end of the 1920s. MPL

CAMPBELL'S RUTHLESS RIPOSTE

Like Segrave, Campbell believed that Daytona was the only option for record-breaking now the target had exceeded 200mph. If Blue Bird hadn't been undergoing yet another extensive and costly rebuild there's every chance its driver would have been on the next ship to the American east coast, but as it was the work lasted for most of 1927 and the Napier-powered icon wasn't ready until the start of the next year.

By that time, US interest in LSR activity had been reignited now that the AIACR would recognise attempts in the country as official. The organisers and promoters behind the course had also cottoned on and, with 1928 representing a quarter-century of speed trials on the famous stretch of beach, a 25th anniversary Speed Meet was convened – Malcolm Campbell and Blue Bird would be its star attractions.

They came from far and wide to see the fastest cars the world had to offer in a variety of categories, but unfortunately the weather gods hadn't read the script as winds caused crashing waves, leaving the sand littered with ridges and gullies. Not known for his patience, Campbell arrived on February 12 and was able to contain himself for just five days. He should have waited longer, because while running at 180mph in a test he hit a bump that propelled his car some 30 feet into the air.

Three days of repairs and he was back out on Sunday, February 19 for a high-speed test. There was no improvement in the weather or on the ground, but thousands of onlookers had filled the temporary stands just in case something special occurred. Something special is exactly what they were treated to.

Blue Bird let out a distinctive roar as Campbell opened up the throttle on approach to the course markers, and suddenly this fast test had turned into the start of a genuine record run. His first pass had seemed quick, and was later revealed to be an incredible 214mph one-way blast – but it had ended badly as the car hit a dune and caused a huge skid that Campbell just had to ride out.

He was meant to stop in between passes for a change of tyres but, whether running on pure adrenaline or shaken by his dangerous slide, Campbell turned almost immediately to make the required return.

The speed into the wind was a fraction under 200mph, his tyres somehow holding on, and the resulting average was 206.96mph. Yet again Campbell had risen up and overcome a seemingly insurmountable challenge – not for the last time.

There were two other serious contenders that had arrived at Daytona along with Campbell in 1928 – they were two very different Americans in two very different cars.

Frank Lockhart's Stutz was an exquisite specimen, scientifically engineered and the smallest LSR vehicle to appear in a generation. It weighed in at just 1270kg, and housed a supercharged 16-cylinder engine of a mere three litres – yes, it gave 385hp, but surely there was no way it could compete.

At the other end of the scale was Ray Keech's Triplex Special, a mighty beast of a vehicle that somehow was home to three 12-cylinder, 27-litre Liberty aircraft units resulting in a total capacity of 81 litres.

The day after Campbell had regained the land speed record, the bad weather cleared and so these two polar opposites took centre stage in a classic David versus Goliath duel.

The 25-year-old Lockhart was first to go. Young he may have been, but he could boast a win at the famed Indianapolis 500 race to his name, and was keen to impress. Technical problems with his supercharger meant much of his allotted time on the course was spent making adjustments, and with only two hours remaining a soft rain began to fall.

Visibility was limited, but Lockhart was not going to miss his chance and accelerated away like a bullet to around 200mph. Not being able to see properly, and because the Stutz was not the stable body it should have been, he suddenly veered left then right before somersaulting into the sea and skipping across the water like a stone.

To the amazement of those who rushed desperately to his aid, when Lockhart was rescued he'd suffered nothing more than a badly cut wrist. He began working on proposed modifications from his hospital bed but his attempts were over for the time being; now it was Keech's turn.

Unfortunately the triple-engine Triplex didn't fare any better. As the four-tonner lumbered across the sand and then gradually built to top speed, a hose in the front engine burst and scalded the driver, who joined his countryman in hospital. The double disappointment brought the 1928 Speed Meet to an end.

Campbell returned to Britain as the record-holder, and the Americans retired to lick their metaphorical wounds and repair their literal ones. Perhaps inspired by their great English rival's determination, both resolved to right the wrongs they had encountered.

Two months later they returned, and this time it was the Triplex up first as Keech arrived at Daytona for another crack. The car performed well, but the timing apparatus failed on the second run – a fast run – meaning the results were void. Keech was incensed, but the only thing he could do was go again.

On the first of two new passes he achieved 210.56mph into a strong wind, then followed that with an impressive 213.90mph with its assistance.

Despite an engine backfire burning his arm, Keech's average for the flying mile was 207.55mph – a slender margin ahead of Campbell, but ahead of him all the same, and the land speed record was back in American hands.

All 81 litres and 36 cylinders having had their say, three days later it was over to Lockhart and his lightweight Black Hawk Stutz to prove their credentials. The Daytona course was in a poor state, but the fearless youngster refused to wait and raced across the wet sand at 203.45mph for a first run. It was an astonishing speed for such a small package, but the return would need to be faster.

At approximately 220mph, Stutz blew a rear tyre – it was the end of its attempt, and sadly it was the end for the brilliant Lockhart who was killed instantly as his car rolled mercilessly across the beach. In the most horrendous of circumstances a great battle had been won, but yet again the world had been given a stark reminder of the perils faced by these intrepid speed merchants who continuously strived to go ever faster and faster.

Frank Lockhart and his Stutz Black Hawk. MPL

Ray Keech brought the LSR crown back to America in the gargantuan Triplex. MPL

The great Henry Segrave and Golden Arrow – a fearsome duo that famously broke the land speed record at Daytona in 1929.
MPL

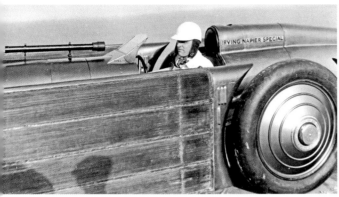

SEGRAVE'S LAST STAND

Unsurprisingly, Campbell was plotting a comeback, but the news that really had the motoring world abuzz was that Segrave was also taking on the challenge of bringing the record back for Britain with an all-new car designed once again by Irving – the creator of the 1000hp Sunbeam. Both men had left the Wolverhampton factory by this time, and had joined forces on the project that they announced would be ready for spring 1929.

The new would-be record-breaker was called the Irving-Napier, named for its designer and maker of its engine, but it became popularly known as Golden Arrow. Encountering little to no hiccups in production, testing or delivery, the car was ready as planned and Daytona was once again selected by Segrave for his third LSR attempt.

Like the project itself, the record campaign ran smoothly and a reserved practice run produced speeds of around 180mph. Segrave then had to wait a fortnight for a disruptive weather system to pass, but he did so safe in the knowledge that when conditions were right his new Golden Arrow had plenty more to give.

When he did eventually take to the course on March 11, a colossal crowd turned out to witness it. Estimates suggested there were up to 120,000 people in attendance, but even if the real number was only half of that it was still mightily impressive.

The expectant crowd was not disappointed either; the first mile was completed in just 15.55 seconds, and although the second pass was slightly slower it was still more than enough to comfortably dethrone Keech and the Triplex and return LSR honours to the UK. Initially the timing was given as a precise 231.36246mph, before it was upped to a final figure of 231.45mph.

Having held the record for nearly a year, Triplex was beaten. However the car emerged the following day, this time with unsanctioned racing driver Lee Bible at the wheel. His runs were quick, but he never really got close to Golden Arrow, and as he strived to find more from the giant machine it lifted off the ground and came down into an uncontrollable skid.

It couldn't be tamed as it began to somersault across the sand, and it ran down a photographer named Charles Traub before unceremoniously dispatching Bible from its clutches. Both men were declared dead at the scene, and Triplex was no more.

Silver Bullet, one of the most promising and ultimately most disappointing cars in LSR history. MPL

CAMPBELL'S DOOMED AFRICAN ADVENTURE

While Segrave triumphed and the land speed record alarmingly claimed more lives, Campbell was in South Africa. He'd gone in search of the 'perfect' course for record-breaking, believing that the weather on the Florida coastline was too unpredictable. It proved to be one of his most ill-fated decisions.

The proposed location was the vast dried lake at Verneuk Pan, and immediately it became apparent that this was not the ideal setting some of Campbell's advisors had professed it to be. First on the list of obstacles was the mud surface, full of sharp shells capable of ripping tyres to shreds – and it didn't end there. Altitude was an issue for the performance of the driver, and at 2500 feet above sea level it would also impact on engine efficiency.

As was his nature, Campbell refused to submit and addressed his problems one by one. Local labourers were brought in to first remove the top layer from a 12-mile stretch across the lake, then to fill it with clay – a much more conducive surface for tyres subjected to immense speeds. Modifications were made to extract more from the engine, and for a short

time it seemed things were back on track.

The setbacks just kept on coming though; Campbell was injured in a light plane crash as he surveyed the course, the team's camp was flooded by the first rain in five years, his wife informed him that frost had burst all the pipes in their Surrey home causing hundreds of pounds of damage, and he was having difficulty arranging transport from Cape Town for Blue Bird. To top it off, news also came through of Golden Arrow's new outright best.

Against all the odds, Campbell did manage to make several record attempts in April and May 1929 – Blue Bird even managing to break the record for the British mile and both the world's five-mile and five-kilometre. But with the altitude resulting in an estimated 11% drop in power, Segrave's new time was never seriously in reach. A new plan was needed.

Sunbeam were the next to make a renewed, but ultimately failed attempt at toppling Segrave. He'd given up land-based record attempts to concentrate on the water, and so Coatalen offered an obvious retort to

Golden Arrow in the form of Silver Bullet – a much-heralded machine with an alleged 4000hp in its arsenal.

Many felt it had a great chance when it arrived at Daytona in March 1930, but it succumbed to engine problems and endured a largely frustrating and miserable time in which driver Kaye Don could only manage a best of 186.05mph. Suddenly a period of incredible success for LSR projects had been replaced by series of high-profile and expensive failures.

Of course Campbell was already back in the hunt, and now he'd turned to a young engineer with a big reputation as he targeted 250mph. That engineer was Reid Railton who, having worked with Parry-Thomas, was no stranger to LSR success. Blue Bird was soon stripped back to its component parts, and Railton prescribed more power by installing a new Napier engine that put out 1450hp at 3600rpm.

Several other changes were made that improved efficiency, durability and streamlining; Railton also working to make Campbell more comfortable at the wheel, reasoning that the driver would be much better placed to achieve greater speeds if he was less

impacted by swerves, leaps and other such outside interference.

On June 13, 1930, news came through during construction that Segrave had been killed while attempting to break the water speed record on Lake Windermere. One can only imagine the emotions Campbell must have felt to lose a respected rival in such a manner, and there are many who in his position would surely have considered calling time on their own careers, believing that luck can only last so long.

But that wasn't how men like Campbell or Segrave were made.

By the following February, Blue Bird was ready. After his chastening experience in South Africa, Campbell returned to the more familiar surroundings of Daytona, where he was about to begin a dominant and unbroken six-year stint as the holder of the land speed record.

Malcolm Campbell and Blue Bird, ready to go again in 1930 after a misadventure in South Africa. MPL

BRILLIANT BLUE BIRD

Looking back there is an inevitability about Campbell and Blue Bird surpassing Segrave and Golden Arrow but, having been brought down to earth with a bump at Verneuk Pan, February 5, 1931, must have been a day of both great relief and sweet success.

Having become used to adversity, Campbell's fifth land speed record was a relatively untroubled affair, completed in less than five minutes.

When the results were collated, he'd achieved an average of 246.09mph – the first time four miles per minute had been broken – and a quite comfortable margin over the previous best.

On returning to England, Campbell was met at Southampton by a celebratory flypast and once docked he was informed that King George V was to make him a knight for his efforts on behalf of the country. He had accomplished every challenge out there, and at the age of 46 there would have been no one that begrudged him a happy retirement. Then again, 246mph was agonisingly close to 250mph.

As the undisputed champion of speed records, the years 1931-1935 were something of a coronation for Campbell. He was rarely given serious competition, and his main endeavour was breaking whatever targets he set for himself. In 1932, with just some small modifications, he took Blue Bird back to Daytona and lifted the outright best to 253.97mph as he began ticking off his personal milestones.

The following year required a little more attention, as the faithful Napier Lion engine was replaced with a new Rolls-Royce V12 R-type supercharged unit – the winner of a major 1931 air race. Increased power meant Daytona's uninterrupted 10-mile stretch was effectively getting shorter, but still Campbell made his annual visit and once again conquered his own mark, this time with his mile average of 272.46mph. The speeds were going up with relative ease, and now almost without warning the previously unthinkable notion of 300mph had come into view.

Targeting this incredible speed, Campbell had a break from LSR activity in 1934, allowing Railton to undertake yet another top-to-toe rebuild of the now legendary Blue Bird. Once again the car returned even better than before, and in 1935 the Daytona sand was laid out in front waiting to be tamed.

Despite yet another record run, this time of 276.82mph, Campbell and his team were left bitterly disappointed. There was no question over the pedigree of the car, the imperious Blue Bird was without doubt capable of a 300mph run. The problem was the course, affected once again by the weather.

Campbell had never been totally at ease at Daytona, despite his unprecedented success there, and now it had become clear that the speeds being aimed for were not possible at the Florida beach. The great man set his sights elsewhere, and a location in the American state of Utah came into focus.

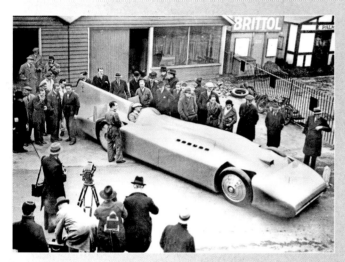

LEFT, BELOW AND ABOVE: A series of images show Malcolm Campbell and Blue Bird at Daytona between 1931 and 1935, a period during which he added four land speed records to his considerable list of accolades. MPL and ✪

aving served with distinction during the First World War, budding engineer and inventor George ET Eyston returned to college after the conflict and began entering car races across Europe. He was not without success, either, as he claimed victory in the 1921 and 1926 French GP.

He also became renowned for his abilities in speed-endurance races, particularly at Brooklands, and his performances led quite naturally to thoughts of conquering the planet's ultimate speed record.

Eyston's first car, Speed of the Wind, lacked the necessary power to reach the absolute top speeds but was more than capable in endurance events. The Oxfordshire man spent another two years conquering various landmarks, but it was Campbell earning the headlines as he lifted the outright mark to more than 300mph. Believing he had the ability to reach such heights himself, Eyston embarked on a project to build a vehicle capable of taking on the world.

The result of his efforts was Thunderbolt, a staggering creation boasting two V12, 36.5-litre engines each capable of putting out 2350hp – far exceeding what Blue Bird, record-holder at time, could manage.

In what would be a trio of record-breaking runs, Eyston bettered Campbell's effort with ease as he took the outright speed to 311.42mph. That mark stood from November 1937 until August the following year, Eyston himself lifting it further to 345.49mph.

A legendary battle then ensued between Eyston and rival John Cobb – and as the latter broke through 350mph for the first time in history it became clear that Thunderbolt was nearing its maximum capabilities. In September 1938, Eyston managed to extract 357.50mph from his prized machine and claim his hat-trick.

His third outright fastest would be his last, however, although it did stand for nearly a year, proving just how formidable Thunderbolt had been. The arrival of the

George **ET Eyston**

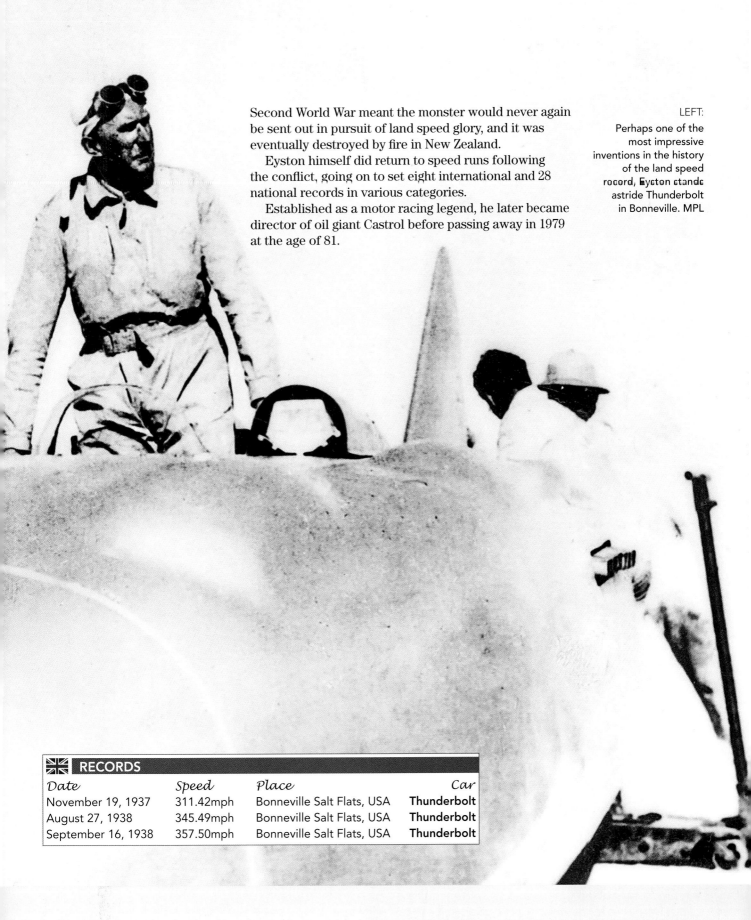

Second World War meant the monster would never again be sent out in pursuit of land speed glory, and it was eventually destroyed by fire in New Zealand.

Eyston himself did return to speed runs following the conflict, going on to set eight international and 28 national records in various categories.

Established as a motor racing legend, he later became director of oil giant Castrol before passing away in 1979 at the age of 81.

LEFT:
Perhaps one of the most impressive inventions in the history of the land speed record, Eyston stands astride Thunderbolt in Bonneville. MPL

RECORDS

Date	Speed	Place	Car
November 19, 1937	311.42mph	Bonneville Salt Flats, USA	**Thunderbolt**
August 27, 1938	345.49mph	Bonneville Salt Flats, USA	**Thunderbolt**
September 16, 1938	357.50mph	Bonneville Salt Flats, USA	**Thunderbolt**

A serial record-setter

John **Cobb**
Brooklands' finest

RECORDS			
Date	*Speed*	*Place*	*Car*
September 15, 1938	350.20mph	Bonneville Salt Flats, USA	**Railton**
August 23, 1939	369.74mph	Bonneville Salt Flats, USA	**Railton Special**
September 16, 1947	394.20mph	Bonneville Salt Flats, USA	**Railton Mobil Special**

J ohn Cobb's road to record breaking took a slightly different path than that of his rivals. With his family home near the famous Brooklands circuit he always had an interest in cars and racing, but the main endeavour in his early adult life was being a director at his father's fur company.

His position had earned him considerable wealth and, when he combined that with the knowledge and experience developed from many years spent working on cars, he was capable of preparing vehicles to achieve speed records. An example of his considerable abilities came in 1935 when he set a new average speed lap record at his beloved Brooklands; the 143.44mph still stands today given that the track was not used for racing after the Second World War.

Cobb was involved in the development of commercial road-going cars, aiming to bring the technology used in speed runs to the manufacturing of safer tyres and better grades of oil. It was not long, however, before his gaze turned to the land speed record.

Working with noted designer Reid Railton, who'd also helped Parry-Thomas and Campbell produce their all-conquering machines, Cobb went to Bonneville in 1938 and became the first man to pass the 350mph milestone to set a new top target. Going toe-to-toe with Eyston, it would take Cobb until 1939 – just a few days before the Second World War began – to once again claim the outright title. He fell just short of 370mph, but was still more than 10mph quicker than the previous best.

Unlike Eyston, Cobb returned to the land speed record scene having served throughout 1939-1945 as an RAF auxiliary pilot. As a new breed of racers explored the possibilities of powering cars with jet engines, the existing record holder set his sights on achieving 400mph before anyone else could and in 1947 headed back to Bonneville for what would be a final tilt.

In both of his attempts, Cobb beat his own top speed – the second yielding 394.20mph and a new land speed record. While the average had fallen just short, he had exceeded 400mph on the return leg of run number two – the first time anyone had done so. A third attempt was briefly considered, but Cobb conceded that the car was at its limit and decided that perhaps discretion was the better part of valour.

Like others before him, Cobb turned his talents to the water speed record and began production of a jet-powered boat he named Crusader. In 1952 he took to the water at Loch Ness in Scotland and posted an average speed of 206.89mph through the measured mile – nearly 30mph quicker than the existing mark.

Regretfully the speed would never become official, as before Cobb could even slow down and turn for the required return run Crusader disintegrated travelling at 210mph and it nosedived into the loch. His body was quickly recovered, but he had sadly lost his life before he was found.

THE BATTLE MOVES TO BONNEVILLE

At the sort of speeds now being achieved, and if Campbell was to realistically threaten 300mph, a new course was needed. The bumps, ripples and soft patches of Daytona were now more than just an unwelcome distraction – at best they were slowing cars down, and at worse they were resulting in driver injuries and death.

Some 1700 miles to the west in the state of Utah was a vast dried lake known as the Bonneville Salt Flats, and it was about to become established as the home of the

land speed record for the next 35 years – and certainly rivalling Daytona as the competition's most iconic venue.

A small town called Wendover had grown around a water supply used to support the building of a railway line in 1909, but apart from that it was a remote area so sizeable that the curvature of the earth is apparent as one looks to the horizon. In summer it's hot and arid, in winter it rains and water sits on top of the salt, never draining and taking days and weeks to evaporate. Bonneville is desolate and unforgiving, an area good for very little but perfect for record-breaking.

As early as 1914, the American 'Terrible' Teddy Tetzlaff had taken a Blitzen Benz to Utah and by stopwatch had narrowly defeated Bob Burman's infamous 141.37mph. As with Burman, the US authorities didn't want to know, the AIACR probably wasn't even aware of it, but the potential was clearly there.

Long-distance records were first challenged on the salt flats in 1932 by another American, Ab Jenkins, who laid out his own circular course. When the Briton John Cobb began taking on international class records there in 1935, it didn't take long before those with eyes on the ultimate prize took notice.

On seeing the alluring white vastness for the first time, Sir Malcolm Campbell was captivated by its possibilities. During an interview in 1933 he had stated: "For my own part, I shall never be happy until I have reached the 300mph mark, and if I am lucky enough to do this, I shall then retire from the arena." Having fallen short at Daytona, here was his chance to bow out in style.

Never one to waste time wondering, Campbell was soon on his way and in late August 1935 Blue Bird arrived at Wendover. Having created a 12-mile stretch with a thick black oil line running through it as a guide, the Englishman eased to 240mph in a test and was confident, as he stepped up on September 3, that his dream speed was in reach.

Entering the measured mile at more than 200mph,

Campbell closed the radiator inlet and almost instantly oil covered his screen and dizzying fumes entered the cockpit. The driver was dazed and initially lost his line; when he found it once more he now had to contend with a burst front tyre. Somehow he held on, and completed the run at 304.31mph.

Apart from a worrying slide as he approached the railway embankment at the end, his second pass was far less eventful and from his rev counter Campbell knew he had passed 300mph – surely he'd achieved his goal. To his intense disappointment and consternation, the timekeepers announced an average speed of 299.87mph.

Having come agonisingly close, he immediately began organising a re-run the following morning; however the day's drama was not over. Two hours later, the chief official of the American Automobile Association stunned Campbell by revealing a mistake in the calculations; the time for the second mile had been given as 12.18 seconds, when in fact it was 12.08 seconds. The two speeds were 304.31mph and 297.95mph – the average was 301.13mph. He had indeed done what he'd promised, although he was furious with the authorities for taking away what should have been a victorious moment.

As he had declared, Campbell did indeed retire after achieving his ninth and final outright best. Despite his annoyance, overcoming the 300mph barrier was the fitting end the greatest LSR career of all time truly deserved.

Sir Malcolm Campbell's Blue Bird takes its bow at Bonneville in 1935. MPL

Thunderbolt leaves the factory ahead of its trip to Bonneville, and Eyston appears in confident mood. MPL

He was known in France as Le Recordman – and it was certainly an appropriate nickname for George Eyston, a serial winner of speed trials and also a fine engineer. It was a formidable combination that took him to hundreds of class records in a variety of cars from Europe and America.

As Campbell retired in 1935 Eyston introduced Speed of the Wind, a larger car designed for top-category long-distance attempts and successful at it. Initially its efforts were in France, but it was soon taking on challenges at Bonneville and inevitably Eyston's thoughts turned to the land speed record. With a growing ambition and the design skill to realise it, when sponsors began making overtures in 1937 he began work on a machine that would come to be called Thunderbolt.

What emerged was the largest petrol-engine record car of them all; seven tons, eight wheels, a 73-litre capacity and an output of 4700rpm.

A shot of the monstrous Thunderbolt from above. MPL

Unlike previous monsters though, it was as attractive as it was large – and with its all-aluminium body shimmering in the desert heat there were gasps of astonishment when it was unveiled at Wendover in early October.

As a man whose trade it was to break records, there were few betting against Eyston at least challenging the now 300mph record but clutch problems meant it was more than a month after his arrival in Utah that his great day finally came.

Thunderbolt was entirely untested when it took to the salt for the first time and although the engine started up without a hitch, Eyston couldn't find a gear and so a full run was abandoned. A heavy rain, flooding and adjustments to the gearing system delayed any further activity for a fortnight, but then came success on October 28 with a timed run across 10 miles producing a speed of 309.60mph. Had a similar mark been achieved on the return, Eyston would have

captured the record but once again gremlins struck and the clutch failed. It was the same story a week later with a first run of 310.68mph, before a broken clutch again prevented a second pass.

Frustrated, Eyston instructed two Los Angeles-based engineers to make new components to his specification and when the parts arrived he was ready to go again. By this time it was November 19, and Bonneville's infamous winter weather was just a matter of days away.

At dawn, the flying kilometre was completed at 305.59mh – not amazing, but in the hunt. This time there were no difficulties at the turnaround as the wheels were replaced and Thunderbolt refuelled in less than 16 minutes ready for Eyston to crown his incredible record haul.

Visibility was poor as the rain loomed overhead, and the silver monster was lost in the whiteness of the course as it blasted into the distance. If the first pass was slightly disappointing, a sensational 319.11mph on the second more than made up for it. At a kilometre-average of 312mph exactly, the land speed record belonged to Eyston and Thunderbolt.

Just 30 minutes later the weather finally broke, and the first rain and snow of the winter season began to fall on Bonneville. Record breaking was over for another year but Eyston, knowing his creation was capable of more, vowed to return the following summer.

Cobb made his name at Brooklands, holding several of the course's own records. He's pictured at the Weybridge track in 1934. Press Association

EYSTON AND COBB GO HEAD TO HEAD

Reid Railton had been the engineering brains behind Parry-Thomas's two land speed records, and had also been employed by Campbell to refresh Blue Bird for its 300mph run. However his long-held desire was to create a car from scratch and when Brooklands expert John Cobb decided to rival Eyston for the absolute best speed in the world, he seized the opportunity.

To challenge the giant Thunderbolt, Railton embarked on the building of a vehicle nearly half its weight – and as with the early versions of Blue Bird it would be powered by Napier aviation engines, two of them in fact. The body was beautiful and perfectly contoured, designed as a detachable shell for ease of access to the components underneath.

In the summer of 1938, the two British cars and their two British drivers descended on Bonneville together. Both were aiming to leave with the land speed record, but only one could, and an exciting battle resembling the days of Chasseloup-Laubat and Jenatzy, or Thomas and Eldridge, became a tantalising proposition.

Eyston arrived first in July, although bad weather meant it was August 24 before he was able to make a genuine LSR attempt. When he did, he produced a shattering first run of 347.16mph and suddenly Bonneville was starting to yield some

John Cobb. MPL

truly remarkable times. The second run seemed even quicker, but a combination of the incredible speed and Thunderbolt's silver paintwork meant the electric signalling failed to register the car passing through it.

Renowned for his level-headedness, Eyston remained calm and waited patiently for three days before returning to the salt. The timekeepers suggested painting the sides of the car in matt black to avoid a repeat, and this time there were no such issues. The kilometre average was 345.21mph, the mile 345.49mph – his own record obliterated by 33mph.

Like Eyston the year before, Cobb

George Eyston. MPL

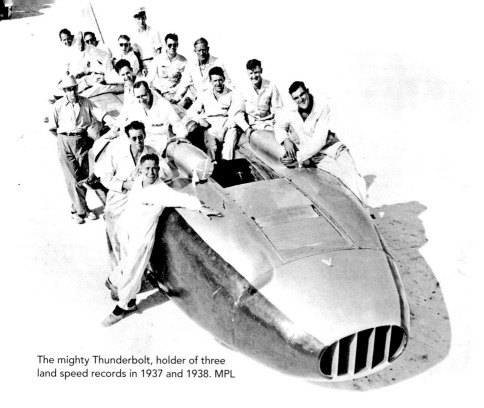

The mighty Thunderbolt, holder of three land speed records in 1937 and 1938. MPL

had work to do in terms of testing and adjustments before he could make a full-blooded run. He put in several test runs and following each of them Railton worked on minor faults and teething issues. By September 12 the team were ready for a proper assault.

A trouble-free attempt produced an average of 342.50mh – more than 100mph faster than what had been possible at the start of the decade but now not enough to claim the outright best. Cobb was pragmatic, and knew that his Railton was capable of more than this first effort had shown.

Three days later he was out again, and in another textbook campaign he ran at 353.30mph on the way out

and 347.20mph for his return. Eyston, who was watching, uttered the words "John's got it" and he was not wrong. Only three years since Campbell had poured so much time, effort and resource into edging past 300mph, the outright best had now surpassed 350mph – 350.20mph to be precise – and another name had been added to the LSR roll of honour.

Even before Cobb had made his September run, Eyston was already working on Thunderbolt in anticipation of his time being overhauled. His remark as Cobb blasted to glory was perhaps not a reflection of how fast he'd gone, but a pre-determined acceptance of

the driver's skills – and those of his engineer Railton.

The main change was the removal of the car's radiator, replaced with a cooling tank, to improve aerodynamics. This was followed by the removal of the tailfin, again for better streamlining, and it says much for Eyston's wide-ranging abilities that he was able to alter Thunderbolt in such a way while 'on the road'.

He was out on the flats the following morning, and after some token preliminary runs began a full-speed attempt to take his record back. The whole campaign lasted just four minutes and passed in the blink of an eye, as did Thunderbolt – 10.10 seconds for his first mile and 10.40 seconds for the follow-up meant Cobb was in possession for less than 24 hours, and Eyston had the last word of 1938.

Every last morsel of power had been eked from the silver monster, and for now it had held off its smaller rival. Cobb and Railton, however, were aiming higher and had 400mph in their sights – they'd just have to wait a year before having another crack.

BEFORE AND AFTER THE SECOND WORLD WAR

The Cobb-Railton combination did indeed return in 1939, without Eyston this time, and with the threat of the century's second major conflict looming large there was a feeling that this might be the last record-breaking season for the foreseeable future.

With the course in near-perfect condition and with little fuss from his exquisitely efficient Railton vehicle, Cobb blitzed to the first ever sub 10-second mile runs on both passes – but it was his kilometre speeds that were fastest and gave an average of 369.74mph.

Once again the record was his, yet once again it was reckoned that more could come from the car. Modifications were needed and so Cobb and Railton called time and returned to England. It'd be nearly a decade before they'd return.

The Second World War came and went, as the land speed record paled into insignificance when compared to the horrors endured in Europe, Africa and across the Pacific Theatre. When life returned to something like normal, thoughts again turned to more entertaining activities and the pursuit of 400mph in a car came back into focus.

A strain on resources meant no new projects emerged in the immediate aftermath, so Cobb brought the Railton out of retirement in 1947 and his great engineer set about making it ready to take on the daunting target.

In August, the team arrived at

Cobb's Railton special was much smaller than its rival, but certainly no less fast. In fact, as Thunderbolt reached what seemed to be its capacity, Cobb's machine seemed to have plenty left in the tank. MPL

Bonneville only to find the usually smooth surface in poor condition with deep holes – albeit filled and rolled – making themselves known when driven over at anything exceeding 300mph. Then, during testing, the Railton began to show signs of its age as old carburation problems resurfaced.

It was September 14 before Cobb could make an attempt on his own record, and the signs when he did were that it could certainly be broken but perhaps 400mph was a challenge too far. His first run was 375.32mph, but the bumpy course damaged

bodywork and Cobb decided against a return. A second effort two days later brought 385.65mph from the initial pass, and then on the follow-up he showed a glimpse of what the Railton could really do with an electrifying 403.14mph.

The average was 394.20mph, Britain had another land speed record and Cobb had his third. The final run had shown that on a smoother course he could have threatened 400mph, but there was little he could do about that. Neither could he control the weather, as rains arrived early at Bonneville to cause flooding and bring a premature end to the season.

Cobb and Railton reluctantly conceded that their veteran machine had run its last race and, content with his LSR career, the driver turned his attentions to the water. As it transpired, Cobb's record would last an incredible 16 years in what proved to be a rather quiet time in the speed scene. But when competition did return in earnest, the introduction of the jet engine brought speeds of well above 400mph into contention.

The veteran Railton was brought out again after the Second World War, and managed to lift its own land speed record – although it ultimately fell short of the 400mph target. MPL

Craig **Breedlove**

here is little doubt that American Craig Breedlove is one of the most enigmatic personalities to ever grace the land speed record arena. And not only has he been one of the most unforgettable characters the scene has ever produced, but he is the man responsible for bringing the pursuit of the ultimate speed prize into the modern era of jet power and rocket propulsion.

Born in 1937, the Californian grew up at a time when the USA was the land of opportunity and the rapid development of technology meant anything seemed possible. With vehicles of all types capable of increasingly impressive speeds, Breedlove – who'd worked for the Douglas aircraft company in his early 20s – believed that Cobb's time could be challenged. In fact, the more he studied the more he came to support the idea of significantly higher speeds being within reach.

Obsessed with becoming the fastest man on earth, he gave little regard to rules, regulations and conventions

and began construction of a three-wheeled machine propelled by a surplus J-47 military aviation jet engine.

After more than a year of development, Breedlove took Spirit of America on to the salt at Bonneville in 1963 and obliterated Cobb's 16-year-old effort to record a comfortable two-way average of 407.45mph – at one point clocking a staggering 426.43mph.

The land speed record had returned to the USA for the first time since 1929, and Breedlove had achieved his dream – or so he thought. With the car possessing only three wheels, and with none of those wheels driven directly by the engine, the governing bodies refused to sanction the time and excluded it from the record books.

A period of chaos and confusion reigned. First there were three separate top speeds established depending on the type of car used, but eventually it was determined there should only be one fastest time, and the best from across the three categories would be officially recognised as the outright land speed record. The

A game changer

decision meant the age of jet power had well and truly arrived. Breedlove's original record-breaking run was belatedly accepted, and both during and shortly after the debate over rule changes he set a further four speeds that counted as outright efforts. He was also responsible for the first speeds higher than 400mph (unofficially), 450mph, 500mph, 550mph and 600mph – a remarkable leap in one of the record's most exciting periods.

As is perhaps evidenced by his desire to push the limits of how fast a land-based vehicle could actually travel, Breedlove was very much the daredevil and was fortunate to walk away from several high-speed, high-impact crashes.

Despite the obvious risks he has continued his affinity with the land speed record both as a driver and a latterly as a team manager, and rumours persist that he's working on a new supersonic Spirit of America capable of more than 1000mph.

ABOVE:
Breedlove poses proudly next to his great creation, Spirit of America. MPL

🇺🇸 RECORDS

Date	Speed	Place	Car
August 5, 1963	407.45mph	Bonneville Salt Flats, USA	**Spirit of America**
October 13, 1964	468.72mph	Bonneville Salt Flats, USA	**Spirit of America**
October 15, 1964	526.28mph	Bonneville Salt Flats, USA	**Spirit of America**
November 2, 1965	555.48mph	Bonneville Salt Flats, USA	**Spirit of America Sonic 1**
November 15, 1965	600.60mph	Bonneville Salt Flats, USA	**Spirit of America Sonic 1**

Donald Campbell was a 26-year-old when his legendary father Malcolm passed away. While the son had an interest in engineering and racing prior to his father's death, it was only after that he began to seriously pursue creating his own legacy.

It took nearly seven years of development, but Campbell junior realised his first dream by setting a new outright water speed record at Ullswater in the Lake District in 1955 with a speed of 202.32mph. He followed that over the course of the next decade by either lifting or breaking the top mark a further six times, eventually ending with a best effort of 276.33mph in December 1964.

The last of these, set at Lake Dumbleyung in Australia, was doubly special as he became the first and so far only man to establish both water and land speed records in the same year.

It was a feat he achieved after turning his attentions to land-based runs at the start of the 1960s, although he had originally toyed with the record at the end of the previous decade only to be injured in a heavy crash. While the accident occurred at a dangerously fast 360mph, such speeds were never going to seriously challenge Cobb's existing mark; with the vehicle destroyed the team vowed to rebuild and return with a monster capable of eclipsing 400mph.

The poor quality of the salt at Bonneville meant the iconic American course was ruled out as being suitable for the new Bluebird – the younger Campbell continuing the famous name of his father's cars – and so Lake Eyre in Australia was selected as the setting for a new assault.

Rain hadn't fallen there for nine years as 1962 dawned, but after a few low-speed test runs severe storms arrived and washed out any chance Campbell had of making history. The salt bed was still partially flooded in July of 1964, but the driver ignored the risks to post a time of 403.10mph in less-than-ideal conditions.

Breedlove's better effort had come a year earlier, and while not official it was widely considered by the motoring community as a legitimate mark. Despite achieving his dream of passing 400mph, Campbell was disappointed with his time generally considering he'd reached a peak speed of nearly 450mph, and specifically because he had been unable to eliminate Breedlove from the equation. Nevertheless, history showed that he had established a new land speed record.

Despite beginning 1965 as officially the fastest man on Earth, and the undisputed fastest man on water, Campbell refused to consider retirement. Instead he commissioned the design of a car capable of going faster than the speed of sound, and he also set his sights on reaching the magical 300mph mark on water. An attempt at the water record would come first but, like many speed heroes before him, he would pay the ultimate price for his continued pursuit of glory.

On the morning of January 4, 1967, he powered through the measured kilometre at 297mph – and just a few miles per hour more on the second run would produce the average he so desired. For reasons that remain unclear, rather than stopping to refuel he immediately turned the boat around and started his second pass. There are many theories as to what caused the events of the subsequent few minutes, but the outcome was tragic. At a speed of more than 300mph, Bluebird lifted into the air and completed a full somersault before smashing back into the lake and disintegrating. Campbell was killed instantly, and another speed king had been lost to the water.

Donald **Campbell**
Destined for greatness

LEFT:
Casually smoking his trusty pipe, Campbell assesses conditions stood in front of the new Bluebird. MPL

RECORDS			
Date	*Speed*	*Place*	*Car*
July 17, 1964	403.10mph	Lake Eyre, Australia	**Bluebird CN7**

A NEW CAMPBELL,
A NEW RIVALRY

Donald Campbell followed in the footsteps of his famous father Sir Malcolm but his first endeavours were on the water, where he made a big impression on the dominant American boat racers, breaking 200mph at Ullswater in the UK. He then went 14mph faster to overhaul his own record on Lake Mead, a stunning effort on US soil.

Whereas many before him had transitioned from land to water, Campbell's ambition was opposite and he left Nevada in 1956 with two main aims – beat 250mph in a boat, and surpass 400mph in a car. The Norris brothers of Sussex, builders of his record-breaking boat, were instructed to begin work on the latter.

Embracing Campbell family tradition, there was no expense to be spared and no compromise to be made – everything would be the best of the best. It's estimated that the cost of his new Proteus Bluebird, named in homage as well as for the aircraft engine it housed, was more than £1 million. Pursuit of the LSR, it seemed, had become a costly business.

While Campbell junior was busy beating his own water record a further four times, the frighteningly powerful new creation was completed and in August 1960 it arrived at Bonneville for what many expected would be a coronation. Four capable American challengers certainly made people think again, one of them housing a

The new-generation Bluebird departs the factory in 1960, ready for a run in Bonneville. MPL

formidable jet engine the like of which would later prove to be Campbell's nemesis.

As each of the competitors went out in turn it was clear that, after a hiatus in the 1950s, the competition for the land speed record was red hot once again and a dramatic month of activity ensued.

*A RECORD IN REVERSE:

Just when it seemed the land speed record was back on a clean and neat timeline, confusion and controversy were about to strike once more. This chapter covers a period from the late 1950s through to 1964 during which, when looking back, it appears the outright best speed 'went backwards'. In fact, the higher of the two speeds achieved during this time wasn't initially recognised as being an official effort, but was generally accepted as such by everyone (this volume included) except for the governing body that made such decisions – therefore explaining the quirk in the evolution of the LSR. This wasn't the only time the record had been disputed, and it wasn't the last, but despite making it somewhat difficult to present a tidy narrative it does serve to provide even more drama to what is an already fascinating tale.

A young Donald Campbell in the cockpit of his father's Blue Bird in 1933. ✪

Local favourite Athol Graham was first to attack the salt in his City of Salt Lake – an inexpensive contender powered by a surplus United States Air Force supercharged V12 Allison aero-engine. A year earlier the car had hit 344.70mph, and there was great interest in whether Graham had made any modifications capable of taking that speed closer to the 400mph required.

Tragically the gathered crowds, made up mainly of the five competing teams, never got the chance to find out as City of Salt Lake veered off the marked course and went sideways. Travelling at more than 300mph, the car catapulted over and over and pummelled itself into scrap – the driver had little chance of survival, and was indeed found dead when rescuers reached him. It was a sombre start, to say the least.

Dr Nathan Ostich came next, with his odd-looking Flying Caduceus – the world's first LSR car powered by a jet engine. While this form of power would go on to dominate the scene, its first incarnation was blighted by technical issues – Ostich's disastrous campaign mercilessly ended when his drag parachute ejected shortly after he began a run. Such were the failures within the car, it's not ridiculous to suggest that its failure to reach high speed may've prevented serious injury or worse. Ultimately, if Ostich had managed a record run it wouldn't have been recognised by the new Fédération Internationale de l'Automobile (FIA) – replacing the AIACR – on the grounds that its wheels were not driven directly by the engine. For now it didn't matter, but as an issue it was far from finished.

But for a broken drive shaft and chain, Mickey Thompson would likely have won back the land speed record for America at Bonneville in 1960. MPL

The blue-painted Challenger 1 of Mickey Thompson showed far more promise than the previous entrants. He first blasted to a run of 372mph, then shocked everyone by improving that to an astonishing 406.60mph – faster than either of Cobb's two passes. If he could make a similar return within the allotted 30 minutes, the land speed record would be back in American hands. He managed to get back on the course in comfortable time, and looked set for glory when a drive shaft and then chain broke. He was so close, yet so far, and the damage meant his effort was over.

Barely had the dust settled when Art Arfons appeared with his first Green Monster. His time was to come at Bonneville, but it wasn't now, and after a probing run of just 249.57mph coupled with technical issues he realised his car was not yet of the class required and withdrew. And that left Campbell.

He made several experimental runs in the beautiful new Bluebird – 120mph, 170mph, 175mph, 240mph – and appeared to be easing towards a full-on effort. Perhaps demonstrating the same impatient nature as his father, on his fifth run he accelerated much harder and was quickly up to around 350mph – but had pushed too fast, too early.

The resulting accident was scarily similar to Graham's, as the million-pound car was strewn across Bonneville's unforgiving desert and crumpled into a virtual write-off. Somehow the driver survived, but did suffer a cracked skull, pierced eardrum and multiple cuts and abrasions. On regaining consciousness in hospital, Campbell's first concern was how soon Bluebird could be rebuilt.

Somehow Bluebird was recovered and reinvented, but Campbell was no longer an advocate of record-breaking at Bonneville and set about finding an alternative course for a renewed attack on what was still Cobb's outright best. He embarked on a campaign in Australia dogged by a variety of obstacles and, before he was in a position to genuinely challenge, a rebellious American came from nowhere to turn the LSR arena on its head. That American was Craig Breedlove, who burst on to the scene with the world's first run of more than 400mph – something he'd achieved with apparent ease on the Utah salt Campbell now despised.

His road to greatness began with a devotion to going fast, a by-product of his life as a drag racer. Breaking the land speed record soon became an aim, and it quickly turned into a lifelong ambition that exists to this day.

First he needed a car and, in the true spirit of the American dream, he began building one in his backyard. He took a simple approach, and because jet power provided the most potential for speed it was jet power that Breedlove chose – specifically a surplus General Electric J47 aircraft unit. Aerodynamics experts assisted with design, scale models were tested in wind tunnels, and after a series of updates and improvements he was ready to turn the proposed project into an actual one. Notably, and importantly in the years to come, the final design only had three wheels.

Money soon dried up, but his knowledge and enthusiasm convinced both Shell and Goodyear to come on board as sponsors providing substantial financial backing and PR power. None of the parties seemed

concerned with the fact the car, neither with four wheels nor with any of those wheels driven by the engine, would not meet FIA standards for the land speed record. Breedlove simply pushed on regardless, his only interest being to achieve a faster average than Cobb over two measured runs.

Testing began at the start of 1962 and showed promise. Some issues needed to be addressed, and they were – the final form being a unique three-ton, three-wheeler that appeared to be simply a grounded jet fighter with its undercarriage down and its wings removed. Aptly, it was christened Spirit of America.

Wherever one comes down on the issue of whether the new contender could truly be called a car or not, few would argue with its aesthetic beauty, and it was far removed from the home-made venture it began its life as when Breedlove took it out on to the salt at dawn on August 5, 1963.

There was an element of rock 'n' roll about the 26-year-old Breedlove and his T-shirted mechanics, and it could be felt throughout his approach as he took the engine up to 90% of its maximum 4000lb of thrust and then released the brakes. It was certainly a show, and suddenly Spirit of America burst away for an untroubled run of 388.47mph. He'd need to go faster, but the car had more.

Using 95% of the J47's power for the second run, the blue-and-white projectile hurtled across the course at 428.37mph – comfortably the fastest single run ever made – to produce an average of 407.45mph. It'd been more than 20 years, before the start of the Second World War, since Cobb had first dared to dream of more than 400mph and now it was a reality.

The timing was precise and the two-way format had been followed to the letter; no one could deny that Breedlove had just driven faster across land than anyone had ever been able to before. A land speed record, however, was not forthcoming.

Primarily, the issue was with Spirit's three wheels and the fact the FIA didn't recognise it as a car – and according to its rules only a car could hold the outright top speed. Rumbling underneath though was the issue of whether a vehicle's engine directly drove its wheels. For a new and carefree generation of enthusiasts, the final number was the only thing that mattered. The purists and traditionalists, of which there were many within the halls of power at the FIA, saw it differently and maintained that Breedlove's creation was essentially a plane bouncing along the ground. Using the three/four wheel argument allowed the organisation to avoid being drawn into a debate, but it certainly would have to deal with it sooner rather than later.

The Fédération Internationale de Motocyclisme (FIM) was only too happy to accept jet power into its record books, and announced Spirit's run as an official tricycle world record. As with some of his countrymen before him, Breedlove was also rather dismissive of what was official and what wasn't – he'd driven fastest, and that was that. There were few who could put forward a convincing counter argument, and the matter was far from over.

LEFT: Breedlove's wife Lee sits in the Spirit of America's cockpit. A talented driver herself, she'd later take the machine to a women's land speed record. MPL

He was young, energetic and brash. The US loved him, European authorities less so, but no one could deny his talent. Craig Breedlove stands with his controversial three-wheeler Spirit of America at Bonneville. MPL

CAMPBELL AND LAKE EYRE

While Breedlove was challenging authority at Bonneville, Campbell was floundering in the Australian outback. He'd already demonstrated many of his father's qualities – skill, determination, courage and resilience, to name but a few. But Campbell Jr had clearly inherited some of Sir Malcolm's flaws and, having already revealed his impatient nature, his adventure Down Under brought his stubbornness to the fore.

It wasn't long after his life-threatening accident in Utah that Campbell's team uncovered Lake Eyre, a dried-up body of water in the wilderness of Australia some 450 miles inland from Adelaide. It offered a smooth surface, hard underbelly and boundless run-in and run-out distance – but perhaps its greatest asset was that there was no rain. There was no 'season' as there was in America, and the chances of being disrupted or halted by the weather were seen as slim to none. The only downside was access, given that a small sheep and cattle station called Muloorina was the nearest semblance of civilisation – and that was 30 miles away.

When the South Australian government agreed to build a 65-mile road from the town of Marree to Muloorina and then to the lake, the sole problem appeared solved and the team agreed Campbell would use

Bluebird arrives at Lake Eyre. MPL

Fine weather and a superb surface – all seemed fine, but there were significant troubles ahead. MPL

Ever the optimist, or perhaps too stubborn to walk away, Campbell remained confident of getting in a record-breaking run in Australia – and was prepared to wait for the right time. MPL

When the rains came they fell hard, flooding the Bluebird team's camp. MPL

Finally, in poor conditions, Campbell was able to have a genuine crack at the record. Against the odds he managed to beat Cobb's time, but he fell short of Breedlove's unofficial 407mph. Top: Press Association, Below: MPL

the newly found venue for a renewed record bid.

In early 1962, preparations were made to transport Bluebird, along with the necessary personnel and equipment, to Australia – and that's when news came through of rainfall at Lake Eyre. As with Sir Malcolm's doomed effort in South Africa, perhaps fate was not going to allow this new LSR venture to succeed because the rain turned to heavy downpours and flooded the area for more than a year. With the benefit of hindsight, perhaps then would have been the time to seek out pastures new but Campbell refused to relent and in the spring of 1963 the team finally made its long journey around the world. Impossibly, the rains came again. Surely it wouldn't last, it couldn't, but as the main party made camp, the clouds became heavier and floods moved in again.

Finally the weather eased – an alternative course was marked out and Campbell began some exploratory runs through the soft and wet salt. Yet again, the weather turned against him and a huge storm pounded Lake Eyre. Bluebird had to be driven out of the camp in the dead of night to avoid being submerged, and when the team returned the following morning they found various gear and equipment floating in the rain water.

Another year had been washed out, and again the party broke up. The frustration boiled over and some bitter words were exchanged between Campbell, members of the team and some of the sponsors. Not helping matters was the ill-timed news of Breedlove's incredible antics.

There was something resembling despair when Campbell and what remained of his team returned to Australia again in 1964, and incredulously they were met with rain yet again. Every time a new course was laid out, rain and then wind intervened and it was more than a month after arriving that Bluebird was even able to hit the salt for tests. Almost laughably, further bad weather then forced them to give up for several more weeks.

Finally, against all the odds, in July 1964 Campbell and his famous car were able to make a record run. Even then it wasn't without incident, and a couple of efforts were aborted before on the 17th of the month he took advantage of some brief respite to make two courageous passes in damp conditions that produced an average of 403.10mph.

The effort was all the more impressive when it became clear the second pass had been made at 429mph with a top speed of 440mph.

Officially, he was the new holder of the land speed record – but the whole affair was tinged with disappointment. Campbell had failed to eliminate Breedlove from the equation by not beating his mark, even though Bluebird was clearly capable of more. Still, despite facing continued adversity, he had achieved what he set out to by emulating his legendary father and climbing the LSR mountain. He'd also struck one last blow for Great Britain before a prolonged spell of American dominance.

Tom **Green** Stock-car superstar

🇺🇸 RECORDS			
Date	*Speed*	*Place*	*Car*
October 2, 1964	413.20mph	Bonneville Salt Flats, USA	**Wingfoot Express**

BELOW:
Walt Arfons (left) and driver Bobby Tatroe stand alongside Wingfoot Express II. The car was an upgraded version of Wingfoot Express that Green had driven to land speed record glory in October 1964, but perhaps the low-key nature of their project compared to Breedlove and others is the reason why so few pictures of the original incarnation exist. MPL

hen part-time stock car racer Tom Green had a chance meeting with vehicle designer Walt Arfons at a trade fair in 1962, surely neither man would have predicted that just two years later their partnership would have yielded a land speed record.

Little is known about Green's early life, but as an adult he became an engineer and possessed an in-depth knowledge of aerodynamics. Arfons, who was one of the leading exponents of incorporating jet engines into car designs, was impressed with that knowledge during their brief encounter and soon the pair began plotting an assault on the land speed record.

Responsibility for power belonged to Arfons, while Green was in charge of design, and the result was Wingfoot Express – named after Goodyear's winged-foot logo because Green had talked the tyre giant into supporting the project financially.

Arfons was always meant to be the driver, but during vehicle testing he spun out of control and suffered a suspected heart attack. He also suffered permanent damage to tendons in his hand while they were unloading for their first tilt at Bonneville, and with doubts over his fitness Green was chosen to pilot their creation.

Despite having only ever driven at a maximum speed of 130mph, he was soon posting efforts approaching 300mph. The car, however, was not yet ready and engine damage halted their attempt. It was at this time that Breedlove crept in with his first 'unofficial' record-setting mark.

In October 1964, three separate jet-powered American teams converged on Bonneville with lofty aims – Wingfoot Express was one of them, and Green was expected to challenge. Initially he was unable to get much above 300mph, but thanks to some advice from a rival he almost immediately made a run of 406mph meaning Breedlove's 1963 record was in sight.

With light fading, Green gave his engine maximum power off a short approach and roared across the salt at more than 420mph to set a new outright best average of 413.20mph.

The other teams fancied their chances of bettering that, and within three days Green had been defeated. It seemed as if the car had plenty more to give, but Green refused another run and retired from all forms of competitive motor racing.

Arfons was far from done however, and returned to Bonneville the following year with Wingfoot Express II – a monster that showed its prowess by reaching a peak speed of 605mph during a one-way run with new driver Bobby Tatroe in the cockpit.

Unfortunately for the duo, the rockets used on the car needed to be changed before a second run could be made and the time taken exceeded that allowed by official adjudicators. It probably wouldn't have mattered anyway, as by the end of that season Breedlove had taken the record past 600mph.

Arthur Eugene 'Art' Arfons
Taking the battle to Breedlove

Half-brother of Walt, Arthur Eugene Arfons – known commonly as Art – was 10 years older than his sibling, but that didn't stop them from competing against each other, first in drag racing and then in pursuit of the land speed record.

Art was the first to have a serious crack at the landmark, and at that time it was still John Cobb's effort that he had to surpass. Neither he nor Walt were able to get within touching distance and it was Breedlove who took the title back to America – albeit unofficially at first.

The brothers were undeterred, and Walt struck first when Green took his Wingfoot Express to glory. However it had been Art that offered the all-important advice to help Walt and Green extract the additional speed from Wingfoot, and so he promptly got to work and pushed his own car, Green Monster, to 434mph – the first of three land speed records he would ultimately claim.

Green's retirement left Breedlove and Art Arfons as the two main players on the scene, and the pair traded records throughout the rest of the season and during the next – and each was lifting the speed by a considerable margin each time.

A blown tyre on Green Monster meant Arfons's 576.55mph in 1965 was his final effort of the fascinating back-and-forth between the pair, and just a week later Breedlove posted his mammoth 600mph run that proved to be insurmountable for the next half-decade.

Arfons returned in 1966, first unable to get close to Breedlove and then crashing during a run in which he was challenging his great rival's time. He built another car, but it was sold at his wife's insistence and he never again made a land speed record run.

In his later career he concentrated on competitive tractor pulling, with a great degree of success as it turned out; he also exhibited jet-powered cars at exhibitions and drove cars and motorcycles in speed tests at his spiritual home of Bonneville.

He was inducted into the Motorsports Hall of Fame shortly before his death in 2007 at the age of 81.

ABOVE:
Art Arfons stands beside his Green Monster,
the jet car he took to a trio of land speed
records in 1964 and 1965.

After a flurry of records in the first half of the 1960s during the 'jet battles at Bonneville', it was five years before Breedlove's 600mph would be beaten. When it was finally surpassed by drag racer Gary Gabelich, it became the last time the land speed record was broken at the iconic American venue – a course that had produced 16 of the previous 17 outright best runs.

Gabelich began racing when he was still at school, and made his name in competitive drag events as he became the first person to win a jet dragster race with a speed of 250mph. Not able to pay the bills behind the wheel alone, he worked for North American Rockwell (later Rockwell International) as became part of its test programme for the Apollo Program – not with the aim of being an astronaut, but to act as a physical and mental performance monitor. He also volunteered to skydive alongside and photograph the company's first space landing capsules as they were dropped from 30,000 feet.

Without Rockwell's knowledge he continued to race in novelty drag cars, but once his employers learned of his dangerous extra-curricular activities he was issued an ultimatum. He made the bold decision to sacrifice a regular salary and go in pursuit of the land speed record.

As luck would have it, a team known as Reaction Dynamics had been developing a hydrogen peroxide-powered rocket dragster and were searching for a driver – Gabelich's name was in the frame.

Breedlove was offered the ride first, but demanded too much money. Drag racer Chuck Suba was second on the shortlist and agreed terms before he was killed in a Top Fuel event – the fastest category in the sport. It left the way clear for Gabelich, and he signed up without hesitation.

The team made its first runs in 1969, but the results were disappointing. For 12 months the car was fine-tuned, and The Blue Flame was unleashed on the salt flats once more in 1970 with encouraging early signs.

Initially the team was unable to turn the rocket monster around within the legal time limit to make the required second run, but finally on October 28 Gabelich made two passes that complied with the regulations and set an average speed of 622.41mph. Finally, Breedlove had been toppled.

With its aims achieved, Reaction Dynamics decided against running the car again and so Gabelich returned to drag racing as the holder of the land speed record. He also took to the water to race drag boats, and proved just as successful.

After Briton Richard Noble knocked Gabelich from his perch in 1983, he reportedly made initial enquiries as to the possibility of reclaiming his crown. Sadly, he would never get the chance to make it a reality as he died from injuries sustained during a motorcycle accident in January of the following year. He was just 43 years old.

ABOVE:
Gabelich, pictured in the vehicle, believed that monstrous The Blue Flame was capable of breaking the speed of sound. Unfortunately he was never given the opportunity to prove it, and 622.41mph remained its one and only land speed record. MPL

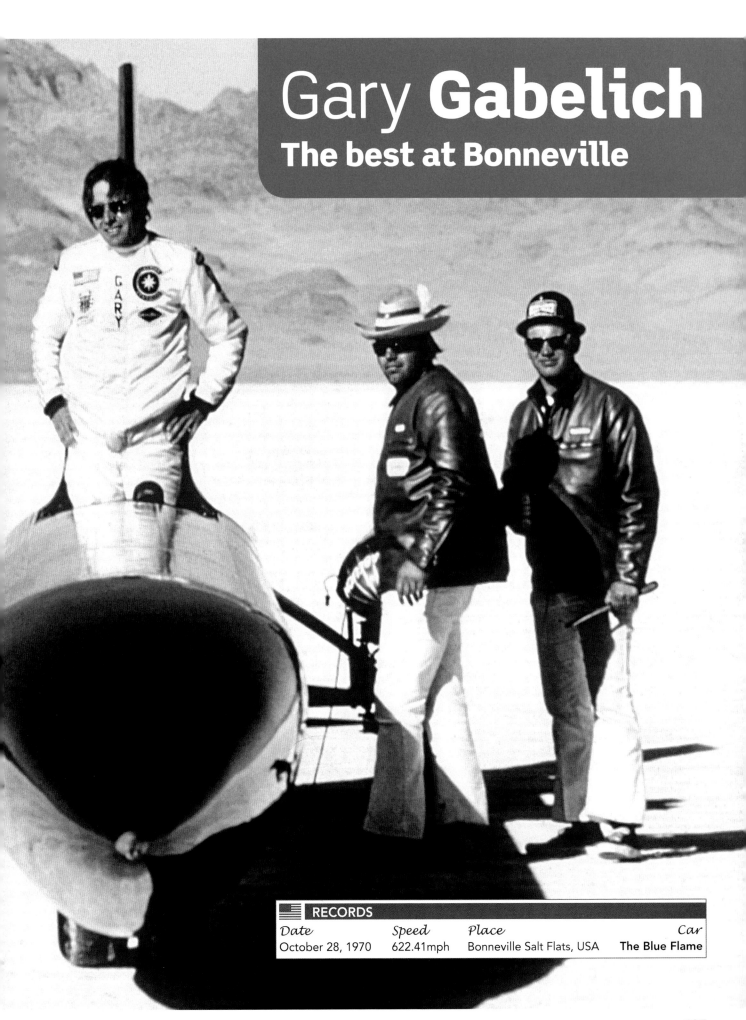

Gary **Gabelich**
The best at Bonneville

One of the few pictures of the original Wingfoot Express, piloted by Green at Bonneville. MPL

Breedlove was far from finished with record-breaking after his exploits in 1963, and returned to challenge the following year. MPL

Art Arfons's incredible Green Monster in action. MPL

SPIRIT OF AMERICA

Donald Campbell had been through two traumatic years trying desperately to make a record run in Australia, only to find that when he did break the official outright best it was largely ignored. While European ignorance to American efforts before the Second World War had just about been successful, the US was now the world's superpower – the FIA could not so easily dismiss attempts made on its soil, especially when those attempts were by American drivers in American cars.

Breedlove led the charge and had been working on upgrades to his three-wheeled jet monster, believing he could quite comfortably better his own time. At the same time, two new jet-powered American challengers had emerged on to the scene – and throughout late 1964 the three took turns in raising the land speed record to a level that left the petrol-powered aircraft engine trailing in their wake.

One of the new pretenders to the crown was Wingfoot Express, built by Walt Arfons. The other was Green Monster, the same to have rivalled Campbell in 1960, built by Walt's younger brother Art. The two projects were entirely separate operations, the two brothers having a frosty relationship and rarely speaking to each other.

Walt was first to go, but not a lot was expected of Wingfoot given its form heading into its Bonneville assault. In testing the year before, the top speed was just 315mph – then the driver Arfons suffered a heart attack, so gallant engineer Tom Green stepped up to the plate. The pair had booked a week at the salt flats, but the indifferent performance left plenty of work to do.

Indeed, a total of 14 runs had yet to yield anything more than 313mph, so on the fourth day Walt and Green fitted a new J46 aviation jet engine. Weather and then fuel pump trouble prevented any initial improvement, but on the sixth day – October 3 – they were finally able to make an impact.

As Green set off, with Walt's instruction to remember the afterburner fresh in his mind, suddenly the bored timekeepers had something to get excited about as Wingfoot did the mile in 406.50mph. It had come from nowhere.

At the turnaround there was some concern about engine damage, but there was nothing that could be done in 30 minutes so Green set about the return in hope more than expectation of the car making it through unscathed. Luck must have been on his side, because with three blasts of the afterburner he made the second pass at a remarkable 420.07mph for an average faster than both Breedlove and Campbell.

Despite there being no love lost with his brother, Art Arfons had actually offered some useful advice to his rivals ahead of their victorious effort. What followed it, however, probably caused further strain between the siblings.

Art's Green Monster housed a mammoth 17,500hp J79 powerplant. It was expertly engineered; it hadn't been expensive to produce but it was not pretty. It had little else at its disposal than raw power, but when it comes to the land speed record there is little else required.

On October 5, just 48 hours after Wingfoot's heroics, Arfons and his Green Monster made a serene pass of 396.30mph one way and then a simply staggering 479mph on the run back. He'd comfortably beaten his brother with an average of 434.02mph, and he'd done it on around 60% power, hinting that there was much more in the locker if and when it was required.

When Craig Breedlove, affronted that not one but two challengers had gone quicker than him, went out on October 13 and put a further 30mph on the world's best speed with an average of 468.72mph, one might have been forgiven for thinking this record-breaking lark was easy. These Americans were truly putting on a spectacular show, and it was not over by a long shot.

Two days later, Breedlove took Spirit out and did it all again – only this time he posted a sensational 526.28mph. No one could believe what they were witnessing on the course and, when Breedlove got into trouble as he attempted to slow following his second run, it was the same story off it.

He had released his drag parachute only for it to break away, and at 500mph there was little chance of his single disc brakes bringing him to a stop. Spirit careered across the salt and finished up in a lake of salt water about five miles away where it was all but submerged. The driver only just escaped drowning but, having wriggled from the cockpit, he managed to swim to dry land and joke that for his next performance he'd set himself on fire.

There was no way the incredible season of 1964 could witness any more drama, or so the conventional wisdom suggested. Still, the year had been anything but conventional and 12 days removed from Breedlove's great escape, Art Arfons was back to show just how much Green Monster had left in reserve.

A bumpy first mile rendered what had suddenly become a tame 515.98mph. That was no problem for Arfons though – he simply upped the power of the huge engine at his command to rocket back over the same bumps at 559.18mph.

The average was 536.71mph – the fifth time a world-best had been achieved in the month. Cobb's masterful 394.20mph had lasted 16 years; in just a matter of days it now stood at nearly 150mph more, and there was little indication that 1965 would be any less eventful or entertaining.

SO, JUST WHO HELD THE LAND SPEED RECORD?

Confused? You wouldn't be the only one, because here were three jet-powered cars (one of them a three-wheeler) claiming to have held the land speed record when neither jet cars nor cars with less than four wheels were eligible for the ultimate speed. Officially, Donald Campbell and Bluebird were still number one, but their speed was more than 100mph slower. This is how it all worked out:

August 1963:
Breedlove sets a world's best time on land, but is ineligible for the land speed record because his Spirit of America has only three wheels. The FIM accepts it as a tricycle world record, while Breedlove and the US authorities openly claim it as a successful LSR attempt.

July 1964:
Campbell breaks Cobb's long-held official land speed record, and is declared holder of the title by the FIA. Breedlove openly rejects this and continues in the belief that he and not Campbell owns the outright best.

October 1964:
Green, Arfons and Campbell exchange five speeds, all of which are faster than anyone has travelled on land before. Because all are achieved by jet power (and Breedlove's with three wheels), the rigid FIA still won't recognise these latest efforts as land speed records under the current definition – but the issue of jet propulsion is not going away and the authority realises it must act.

October 1964:
The FIA creates separate categories for traditional wheel-driven cars, and for non-wheel-driven specials. It then decrees that whichever is the fastest overall speed from both is the official land speed record, thus legitimising all of the recent four-wheel attempts at Bonneville and belatedly recognising Art Arfons's 536.71mph as the record-holder.

December 1964:
At a meeting in Paris, the FIA and FIM agree to recognise the highest speed recorded by either body as the absolute land speed record, meaning the title can go to any vehicle running on any number of wheels, whether wheel-driven or not. It makes no difference to Green Monster's position, but it does mean each of Breedlove's efforts are retrospectively awarded LSR status because they were ratified by the FIM. The FIA upholds its four-wheel minimum.

BREEDLOVE'S YEAR

With clarity at last, the first challenger of 1965 was a familiar name but in a strikingly different car. It was a wild innovation created by Walt Arfons and although it used the same Wingfoot Express name, that's really where the similarities ended. That's because, for the first time, rockets were used to provide the power – several of them in fact.

While the theory was sound, and huge acceleration was possible, the rockets deployed by Arfons weren't capable of lasting the distance and new driver Bobby Tatroe could only muster 476.60mph. It was apparent that Walt wasn't in a position to challenge.

A man who could was Breedlove. It was expected that he'd reappear with a rebuilt three-wheeler, but he'd been working in secret on a new four-wheeled project that had kept the Spirit of America name – but was subtitled Sonic 1.

With a similar General Electric J79 engine to Green Monster, the new design had a theoretical speed of 800mph and Breedlove resolved to put the record out of Art Arfons's reach. When it was unveiled in late October all eyes were on the new monster, but

The second incarnation of Breedlove's incredible car was more impressive than the first, and its rivals simply couldn't match its immense power. MPL

inevitably of a fresh creation there were some teething problems.

One of them was that the front end lifted at speed, and when Sonic 1 was out on a high-speed test run Breedlove had ended up shooting some 1000 feet off the course and ended perilously close to the sight of his salt bath the year previously. Larger nose fins were fitted and re-angled, and on November 2 it went out in search of glory.

Without really extending Sonic's capabilities, Breedlove produced a straightforward run to beat Green Monster with relative ease. His speed through the kilometre of 555.48mph was a new record, and once more a sizeable margin had been added – it seemed the days of lifting speeds by single figures had long since passed.

To little surprise, Arfons plotted an immediate response and soon had his trusty behemoth waiting in the wings ready to strike.

He allowed Breedlove to hold on to his newly won crown for five days, then he calmly headed out to the course and with no preliminary runs

went through the timing traps at an average of 576.55mph for yet another new absolute best. Unfortunately for Arfons, this one did come at something of a price as damage resulting from a burst tyre at 550mph ended his season.

The driver was unhurt, but Green Monster needed work, and if Breedlove could reply then he'd

undoubtedly leave Bonneville as the official record-holder – something he'd never actually managed.

Eight days of limbering up followed, then he was ready; and with a new afterburner in place he was supremely confident of defeating Arfons and being the first man to pass 600mph. On November 15 he achieved that ambition – one run of 593.18mph and a second of 608.20mph.

The average was a resounding 600.60mph, although Sonic 1 had threatened to take off throughout – Breedlove's skill and considerable experience averting disaster.

The weather closed in and ended racing at Bonneville for 1965, and not only did Breedlove have his record for a year but he actually went on to keep it for the next five – challengers throughout the subsequent summers unable to topple him. That was until a new rocket monster came along.

After success with the first Wingfoot, Walt Arfons (standing) came again in 1965 with a rocket-powered machine. It had the speed, but not the durability, so he and driver Bobby Tatroe bowed out of the competition. MPL

In the midst of the intense back-and-forth at Bonneville, few had been given a chance to catch breath and consider what had really happened. By introducing its 'specials' category, the FIA had essentially ended the era of the car in the land speed record – in fact, Donald Campbell's run was the last wheel-driven effort to ever hold the absolute best speed, and although the top effort in the category has been increased since it's never come close to challenging the fastest machines around.

Those machines have developed into largely into grounded aircraft. Engineers have mainly favoured jet engines for these freaks, but in 1965 a trio working out of Milwaukee, Wisconsin, embraced the notion of rocket power.

Their company, Reaction Dynamics, initially produced a smaller drag car – a stunning vehicle that resembled the Formula 1 types of the day. It was entirely powerless as a car, with no method of even starting it – all of its propulsion came from a cylindrical 13-gallon tank mounted vertically behind the driver.

Evidently it was enough, because it covered a standing quarter-mile in just 5.41 seconds – and that was with it coasting through the last 300-or-so feet. Everywhere it went, it defeated its jet rivals and its performances were more than enough to bring sponsors on board for the ultimate aim of building an LSR contender.

Support came from the American natural gas industry, and the car was duly named Blue Flame. When it emerged in 1969 it resembled a missile, and was the longest record car ever produced at that time. Power was an awe-inspiring 35,000hp, yet total weight was only two tons – there was little doubt that if deployed correctly it was going to be capable of incredible speeds, but could the driver control it? What was going to stop it from taking off? These were new obstacles in an era of previously unthinkable velocity.

Technical difficulties and a strike within the American auto industry meant it was September 14, 1970, before Blue Flame and its new driver Gary Gabelich reached Bonneville and began trial runs on the salt. Teething problems were present, of course, but gradually all were overcome and eventually it was recording speeds of close to 600mph – then one considerably above it.

Rocket fuel could only last so long, and so to save valuable seconds the team decided to use a truck to push Blue Flame up to a speed of around 35mph-40mph – the final piece of the puzzle had dropped into place.

A first pass brought a speed of 631.37mph for the kilometre, comfortably the fastest ever recorded. Blue Flame had an hour to make a return pass, but recharging the hydrogen peroxide rockets was a lengthy operation and 48 agonising minutes elapsed before Gabelich and the machine were ready once more.

Off he went, and just a few seconds later it was done and the news came through; his speed was 629.41mph for the kilometre, meaning an average

Stan Barrett and the Budweiser Rocket; not a record-breaker, but perhaps it went faster than anything before. Unfortunately, it now seems we'll never know. MPL

A stunning shot captures the raw power of Blue Flame's rockets as it whips up the salt from the surface below. MPL

STAN BARRETT AND THE BUDWEISER ROCKET

The fascinating tale of the Budweiser Rocket, worthy of its own dedicated coverage, doesn't quite sit within the timeline of the land speed record – but does form an important aside to the narrative presented in these pages. That's because, on the morning of December 17, 1979, it's claimed American Stan Barrett travelled very briefly at the speed of sound in a rocket-fuelled three-wheeler at Rogers Dry Lake.

The campaign, masterminded by speed fanatic Hal Needham, began life as an LSR attempt – but Needham built his creation with maximum power in mind, not to be concerned with lasting a certain distance or completing a return run. Rather than start again, he strapped a 12,000hp booster from a Sidewinder missile to his already incredible vehicle and declared an intention to break the sound barrier instead.

Stuntman Stan Barrett was enlisted as the pilot, Budweiser was brought in as sponsor and the venue at Edwards Air Force Base in California was selected. Temperature was cold on the day, making the weather-dependent speed of sound 731.90mph. Barrett ignited the rocket and activated the missile, it was all over in a flash and attention turned to an array of analytical equipment. The timing trap was examined first, but it had picked up a truck in the distance and returned 38mph. Needham's team then set about unpicking data from the rocket's accelerometer and from radar-tracking – and confidently proclaimed that it had reached a peak speed of 739.67mph for a fraction of a second.

Given that Needham refused to release the information for independent verification, controversy has reigned ever since. No official timing body was present, and there is no record for a singular top speed – the run wasn't eligible for any official recognition, and the way it was undertaken means it's unlikely to have been given it anyway. Furthermore, no sonic boom was witnessed, casting doubt over the findings. Needham passed away in 2013 following a battle with cancer, and the truth probably went with him. But, despite the hotly contested debate about the sound barrier, all the available evidence does suggest the Budweiser Rocket approached and possibly broke through 700mph. It might not have been official – but goodness it was fast.

of 630.39mph and yet another comfortable land speed record.

Content with its work, the team sat back and awaited a new challenger, while continuing to explore how Blue Flame might go even faster. There was now a feeling that the sound barrier was within reach, and the vehicles being produced certainly appeared capable. Whether a human being could control an attempt that fast on land was another matter.

The missile-like Blue Flame prepares to blast across the salt. MPL

Richard **Noble**
Returning the record to Britain

RIGHT:
A young Richard Noble had a dream to be the fastest man on Earth, and at Black Rock Desert in 1983 that dream was realised thanks to his own incredible jet car Thrust2. Driver and vehicle are pictured here. MPL

Donald Campbell's brief reign aside, the USA had dominated the land speed record for more than two decades before Richard Noble and Thrust2 roared across a Nevada desert to claim the title back for the UK.

Not since John Cobb had Britain held the undisputed title, and ironically it was Cobb that had inspired Noble's fascination with speed. Born in 1946, most of his contemporaries grew up on stories of the legendary Sir Malcolm Campbell, but as a youngster Noble had seen Cobb's jet boat first-hand on Loch Ness during a family holiday and soon became obsessed with going fast on land, sea and in the air.

Following that passion he became a pilot after graduating from college, before proving to be something of an entrepreneur – although not necessarily a successful one at first. He backed the development of a light aircraft and a boat known as Atlantic Sprinter, but despite seeming like viable projects both ran into financial trouble. Less likely to ever get off the ground was Farnborough F1, an air taxi service that allowed city workers a route around London's busy transport network.

Speed was still his ultimate dream, however, and when he decided to build a jet car in 1970 he started out on a path that would lead him to unprecedented success. His first creation was basic, and was never intended to break any speed record; instead he planned to use the vehicle to learn effective control at high speeds and build public awareness in an effort to raise funds.

Thrust1 showed promise, but was written off in 1977. Noble though managed to finance a rebuild later the same year, and with sponsors throwing their support behind his plans by the early 1980s the team was ready to seriously challenge Gabelich's now 10-year-old top speed.

Accepted wisdom was to run at Bonneville, and that's exactly what the Thrust unit did. They found, however, that the car couldn't cope with the salt – in any case, poor weather in both 1981 and 1982 meant any genuine attempt was not possible.

Ahead of the following season, Noble had heard about Black Rock Desert in Nevada and on the surface it seemed like the perfect location for Thrust. The team soon established a 13-mile course, and finally Noble was ready to fulfil his lifelong ambition.

Having recaptured the land speed record for his country with his 633.47mph, Noble disbanded the team and pursued numerous other interests. The lure of land speed glory proved too great though, and when Noble

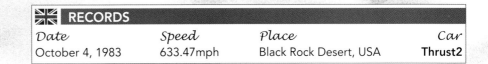

RECORDS			
Date	*Speed*	*Place*	*Car*
October 4, 1983	633.47mph	Black Rock Desert, USA	**Thrust2**

got word of various productions capable of challenging his speed he reignited the Thrust name and launched a team with the intention of developing a supersonic vehicle. When Andy Green piloted ThrustSSC to a gargantuan 763.07mph in 1997, Noble's legacy as both a land speed record driver and successful team figurehead was complete – or so it seemed.

In 2002, Noble vowed that his involvement in the scene was over and he would never return.

But, a mere five years later, rumours began to circulate that he and Green had once again joined forces in a bid to develop the ultimate speed machine. As of 2017 their Bloodhound SSC has transitioned from idea to reality, but it's just one of several vehicles aiming to be the first to break the previously unthinkable 1000mph landmark.

RICHARD NOBLE AND THRUST2

America, fuelled by its pioneering advances across all forms of technology and engineering, had dominated the LSR arena for two decades. If a genuine challenge was to be mounted it was going to take both a special creation and an unrelenting dedication to succeed. Enter Richard Noble.

It had all started back in 1952 when, as a child, he witnessed John Cobb break the water record – an event that later inspired him to build a fast car called Thrust1. In his own words, this first creation was "thoroughly dangerous" and was more of an experiment than a genuine attempt.

He sold it to a scrapyard for £175, and decided that if he wanted to embark on something serious he'd need some engineering expertise. Fortunately he met John Ackroyd.

As it happened, 1979 was a significant year for the land speed record. Needham's wildcard claim to have broken the sound barrier, albeit unsubstantiated, solidified growing belief that such a thing was theoretically possible.

It was also the year that Noble and Ackroyd began work on what would become the next successful LSR project.

Noble, centre, and members of the Thrust2 team in 1982. MPL

NEW VENUE, NEW RECORD

History has proved that the pair were on to something with their idea, but finances were a problem in the early days; the only capital they possessed between them was the money Noble had made from the sale of his first car. Still, it wasn't going to stop them and, in a workshop on the Isle of Wight, Thrust2 started to take shape.

Though Gabelich and then Barrett had demonstrated the capabilities

A look at Thrust2 in 1983, the year of its record run. MPL

of rocket power, Noble and Ackroyd chose a jet engine for their new monster – a single Rolls-Royce Avon powerplant from an English Electric Lightning fighter aircraft. In design and configuration, it bore a striking resemblance to the Green Monster series of Art Arfons.

By 1981 it was ready to go, and following convention the Thrust2 team departed for the salt flats of Bonneville. But, when testing got under way, the vehicle's big wheels and considerable weight hammered

the surface and prevented a smooth run. Noble did manage 500mph to demonstrate the machine's potential, but perhaps the famed Utah course was no longer the appropriate venue – although given the problems that besieged both Sir Malcolm and Donald Campbell it would take a brave man to look elsewhere.

The rains came to end the questions, for that year at least, but the team did return to Bonneville in 1982 – although the weather was so poor Thrust2 didn't even make it off the

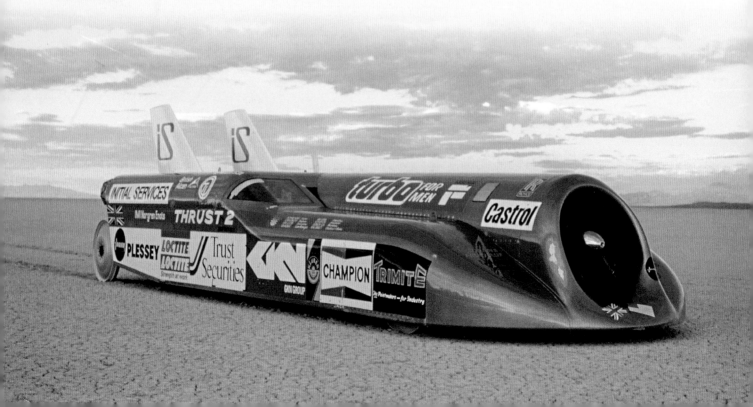

Noble and Thrust2 blast across Black Rock desert in 1983, on their way to a new land speed record. MPL

The car, and its creator. MPL

trailer. With time on his hands, Noble was made aware of Black Rock Desert in the neighbouring state of Nevada. On inspection, he was so impressed with what was essentially a giant mud flat the decision was made to make the record run there in 1983. Third time proved to be a charm, although not without hiccups.

On September 29, 1983, Noble roared down the new 13-mile course at 622.84mph – a similar speed to Gabelich's run some 13 years before. Try as they might, the team couldn't turn the car around in the required time and so the record stayed with the American for now.

One issue that did trouble Noble was how Thrust2 seemed to dig into the desert as speed increased. This downforce needed to be reversed to

take pressure off the wheels, and it was advice from the familiar name of Craig Breedlove that helped achieve what was needed. The team raised the nose slightly, and the results were immediate.

During a first run on October 4, Noble raced to 624mph before returning at 642mph – with a peak speed of slightly higher than 650mph. It all meant that after 20 long years he'd finally wrestled the record back from American hands.

Concerned that should Thrust2 accelerate any more it would take off – not a pleasant experience at 650mph – he called time on the project and stepped back safe in the knowledge he was in possession of the absolute fastest speed. It was by no means his last involvement in LSR activity.

CONTROLLING A LAND SPEED RECORD MONSTER

In 2013, Richard Noble was interviewed by Autocar to mark the 30th anniversary of his record-breaking run. During the conversation he offered a fascinating insight into what it's like driving a jet-powered beast at such tremendous speed:

"You're on a track about 50 feet wide, driving by eye with a marker line on your right. Between zero and 300mph, the car's all over the place, because although Thrust2 has two tail fins, they don't really work until around 300mph, where the car starts to settle. Between 300mph and about 550mph it's a bit boring – more of the same, but faster. Then towards 600mph you start generating a shock wave off the front of the engine; it looks like a mist surrounding the car and is really something to see. It dawns on you that you're going pretty fast.

"Your mental processes speed up so everything happens slowly. You're actually quite relaxed, and even at 650mph you see small details. I remember seeing the tyre tracks the timekeeper's vehicle had left when it crossed the track earlier.

"Then you're into the measured mile, for a few seconds, and then the fun starts. Slowing these cars down isn't easy. You've overstressed and overheated the engine, so you've got to cool it for three seconds – one... two... three... – before you shut off the fuel. That seems an eternity.

"Then you press the parachute button on the steering wheel. There's an instant explosion behind and suddenly you're decelerating at 6g, about 130mph per second. When you get to 400mph, it feels so slow you could get out and walk, but you have to wait for 200mph before you can use the wheel brakes. Then it's time to get it turned around for the return."

Andy **Green**
Feeling supersonic

RECORDS			
Date	*Speed*	*Place*	*Car*
September 25, 1997	714.14mph	Black Rock Desert, USA	**ThrustSSC**
October 15, 1997	763.07mph	Black Rock Desert, USA	**ThrustSSC**

As a former Royal Air Force fighter pilot, Andy Green became accustomed to travelling at extreme speeds during his career – and as such he was no stranger to breaking the sound barrier in the air. It made him the perfect candidate then to pilot Richard Noble's new incarnation of Thrust, and with the millennium approaching the duo set about achieving a historic supersonic land speed record.

First the car was taken to the Jordanian desert for vigorous testing and, despite encountering a series of challenges and setbacks, by the autumn of 1997 the team felt ready to head back to Black Rock in Nevada to both overhaul Noble's own outright best speed and become the first outfit to travel at the speed of sound.

The problems that plagued the vehicle in the Middle East resurfaced in America, but it possessed such sheer power and velocity that once Green opened the throttles ThrustSSC simply could not be tamed. In late September Noble's 14-year-old mark was comprehensively beaten by a phenomenal run of 714.14mph. During neither pass did Green break the sound barrier, but he came tantalisingly close, and the racing season was far from over.

Three weeks later Green once again climbed into the cockpit preparing to put both body and mind through severe trauma in pursuit of land speed immortality. Exactly 50 years and one day since US pilot Chuck Yeager had become the first man to officially fly at the speed of sound, Thrust's shockwave echoed around the mountains as Green made a thunderous first run.

A second measured mile of just 4.7 seconds, complete with another sonic boom rumbling across the desert, lifted the average speed to a dominating 763.07mph – itself only just short of the 768mph sound barrier. Authorities soon confirmed what everyone knew; Green had indeed exceeded the formidable landmark on both the north and south runs. ThrustSSC was officially supersonic.

Green became an international hero, and was promptly honoured with numerous accolades, including being made an OBE and receiving the prestigious Segrave Trophy. His services were in high demand, too, and soon after he returned to the UK he was enlisted by agricultural machinery giant JCB to capture the diesel-powered land speed record that had stood at 236mph since 1973. On August 23, 2008, Green lifted the mark to 350mph, having already broken the record the previous day.

In modern times, Green is unrivalled and unequalled when it comes to feats of speed. Perhaps it's no surprise then that Noble is once again planning to deploy his incredible talents in Bloodhound SSC. There are few who'd bet against Green delivering yet more history.

Driver Andy Green and ThrustSSC in October 1996. Press Association

THE SPEED OF SOUND

Noble's record had not come easily. The FIA required that a new outright best must exceed the previous effort by at least 1% to be recognised; Thrust2's kilometre speed had failed to do this, and it was only the two-way mile run that been successful. Indeed Thrust2 had never actually been intended as a record-breaker, and was always intended as a stepping stone to an even faster car – one that might be capable of travelling at the speed of sound.

After his success at Black Rock, the team figurehead moved on to new challenges, but his LSR interest was reignited in 1990 when he had a chance meeting with Craig Breedlove at Bonneville – the five-time record-holder informing him that he'd purchased two General Electric J79 jet engines and was planning a comeback. It was all the ammunition Noble needed to reignite his original aim of threatening the sound barrier.

With his other pursuits taking up most of his time and resources, it was two years before Noble was able to put actions against the new project. The main event that kicked things off was a meeting with aerodynamics expert Ron Ayers – a man who could help him design his next creation. Ayres sat down with Noble's team manager Ken Norris, the idea of a supersonic car was discussed and the research phase began. From the outset, Ayres

doubted a supersonic land speed record was possible. He was more than willing to explore the possibilities, but believed the shockwaves that would be generated under the car would lift it into the air and rip it to pieces. His major problem was that because no one had come close to it before (Needham and the Budweiser Rocket aside), he had no data or precedent to analyse.

Through a long and rigorous process of complex data modelling, super-computer calculations and scale model testing, Ayres discovered that everything seemed to match up. In fact, there was an unerring accuracy between the actual data he had been able to gather on high-speed vehicles and the predictive data produced by the technology at his command. Designers, engineers and sponsors gave the go-ahead, and Noble named the new project ThrustSSC – for Thrust Supersonic Car.

Specialist racing car builder G-Force Engineering was contracted to produce the 54-foot long, 12-foot wide giant, and as the expansive wealth of components was added it began to take shape. With something to show, Noble was able to begin a large-scale fundraising campaign. He was a successful businessman, but not wealthy enough to finance such an assault on the LSR himself and would need to find ways of generating much-needed cash.

THRUSTSSC ON THE ROAD

To generate interest in the project, and gather support for a supersonic bid, the car was displayed at various events around the country – museum open days, motoring shows and other specially arranged exhibitions where enthusiasts and the public could catch a glimpse.

Testing was also a requirement now, and would take place in a series of stages – installed engine tests, full reheat engine tests, low-speed runway tests and full reheat runway tests. Once that was finished, ThrustSSC was scheduled to go to the Al-Jafr Desert in Jordan for some genuine speed runs.

As preparations continued in the Middle East in mid-1996, it was summer in England and sponsors began to throw their weight behind the new car as it took to the Tarmac at Farnborough Airport for the first time. Initial forays were aborted at the last minute, with minor problems halting progress – one such effort being called off with the car ready at the end of the runway with its two huge afterburning Rolls-Royce Spey jet engines already rolling. When the problems were finally overcome the 10-ton machine moved under its own power for the first time – that power having been underestimated as both front tyres burst from the extreme pressure. Serious progress was not far behind, as five runs were made in one

The car took with it a full-time team of mechanics and engineers wherever it went, and there were few occasions when adjustments or just regular checks were not being made. Jeremy Davey, SSC

day alone before the event concluded with a 200mph effort on full reheat.

A media call was scheduled to showcase ThrustSSC to even more would-be sponsors and backers as the team packed up the array of supporting equipment for its trip to the Jordanian desert. At the same time, news emerged that Breedlove had begun making runs at Bonneville in his Spirit of America Formula Shell LSRV creation. The race to the sound barrier was well and truly on.

With a series of teething problems ironed out, and the engines showing promise, the time had come to run ThrustSSC at something close to record speed – although an attempt on Noble's own 633.47mph was unlikely in the short Al-Jafr Desert. In fact, the team's new driver Andy Green would not have the chance to get close.

The first problem encountered was the stones scattered across the course.

Thousands of hours would be required to manually remove them, and while that problem was being tackled the mechanics revealed a variety of further issues with ThrustSSC's internals – nothing catastrophic, but all time-consuming.

Two weeks after arriving at its new camp, the team was ready to let the beast out of its cage and a quick 260mph dash blew off the cobwebs and set the scene for a steady increase towards 700mph. But as those speeds got faster, the solidity and bumpiness of the surface was causing damage to the steering mechanisms and more precious days were spent repairing the problems and ironing out the causes.

Poor weather then came and went to cause even further delays, and though the steering geometry had been altered and damping increased, the team wasn't able to test the modifications due to a night of torrential rain that arrived to breathe life back into the hundreds of tributaries that ran from the surrounding hills down into the desert. The camp had to be evacuated, and testing was over for 1996.

Noble and his team had learned much from their venture to Jordan, but had little in the way of demonstrable results – particularly in the form of impressive speeds. Sponsors were nervous and, with funds still needed to get the team out to Nevada, it was going to take some skill to convince potential backers to part with even more money.

ThrustSSC's dedicated team. Matt Cole, SSC

Had it been anyone else but Noble, his LSR credentials clear for all to see, at that point the team might have folded with its dream tantalisingly out of reach. This, however, was a man who'd become the fastest in the world in 1983 starting on a budget of just £175 – being stopped in his tracks by an obstacle like lack of finances was not an option.

Late 1996 and early 1997 were all about preparation for Thrust SSC, preparation for a return to Jordan to finish a comprehensive and much-needed testing process. A specially chartered air-freighter flew the car, equipment and various team members back to Al-Jafr in summer 1997, and it took just a day for them to get ThrustSSC into action with a 130mph run just to ensure all was in good working order.

Everything checked out, and the car was prepared for the next runs before a dust storm moved in and forced a hiatus – it was a case of one step forward, one step back. The next problem was the rising temperatures; the morning window to head out on to the course was getting tighter and tighter and the intense afternoon heats were causing damage to the engine and electrics.

ThrustSSC is tested at Farnborough in August 1997. It had undergone a similar workout at the same location the previous year. Press Association

ThrustSSC was up against a familiar name in Spirit of America, seen here running at Black Rock in September 1997. Jeremy Davey, SSC

Working quickly, the team put in two runs to a peak of 300mph, and then a day later ThrustSSC hit 430mph – a couple of engineering days, and some speeds in excess of 500mph would be possible. Yet again they were thwarted; more damage and more repairs came and went and then finally the team had a breakthrough with a trouble-free pass of 540mph. Well, trouble-free it seemed, but on subsequent inspection a suspension bracket had broken – an issue that would take two weeks to put right.

The desert heat was rising even further, and with the rough course still causing issues, staying to pursue the 600mph target was deemed unwise. There was nothing more that could be done in Jordan, and it was time to take ThrustSSC to Nevada and line up against Breedlove's new Spirit of America team in a fascinating supersonic showdown.

SHOCKWAVES ECHO AROUND THE MOUNTAINS

Just weeks after leaving Jordan to return to the UK, Noble, Green and the ThrustSSC team arrived at Black Rock Desert in good shape, and quickly set up camp. Spirit of America took an early lead with its car ready to run first, but the British outfit quickly showed it was much further along the difficult testing and development process before hitting repeated problems with its computer systems. The Americans, meanwhile, had to change engine after the installed J79 powerplant ingested a foreign object – it was a major setback.

ThrustSSC motored on, and on September 25, 1997, struck a decisive blow as Green set a new absolute land speed record with a blistering run of 714.14mph. Noble's own creation had beaten his 14-year-old effort, and a new Englishman had stamped his name on the history of the famous competition. On a wider note, in just less than a century, the record had increased by a staggering 1720% – if only Chasseloup-Laubat could have been there to witness it.

Breedlove and Spirit of America would never recover, and beset by problems with the replacement engine he could only reach around 340mph – nowhere near the standard required. Noble and Green showed little mercy, consistently adding to the world record in test runs. However they weren't interested in small increases to the officially recorded outright best; they were targeting a run at the speed of sound.

On October 13, the sonic boom echoed around the desert during a fully timed run through the measured mile, but the return run began an agonising 49.6 seconds after the allotted hour and so Green and ThrustSSC were denied the first supersonic land speed record. They still had time.

Two days later and the car was back in action, and this time achieved the goal its creator so desired. Going out at 759.33mph, Green came back even faster and produced a scintillating average of 760.34mph for the kilometre and 763.07mph – the latter becoming another new land speed record. Most significantly the sound barrier was broken during both the north and south runs, reaching a maximum of Mach 1.020. It was a simply breathtaking day, and it sparked jubilant scenes.

With the mission accomplished, the car and team returned home to

Two stunning images show ThrustSSC at speed across the desert. Duncan Garrett and Rod Barker, SSC

ThrustSSC roars across Black Rock desert, claiming a second land speed record and becoming the first to break the sound barrier. Jeremy Davey, SSC

a hero's welcome; there were TV appearances, events and even an invitation to the Lord Mayor's Show. Green was made an OBE for his achievements, and joined the likes of both Campbells, Segrave, Cobb and Parry-Thomas as Britain's finest exponents of speed.

For others the question was, what next? Given the time, effort and considerable budget now required to take on the land speed record there was simply no point in going through the process for a mere few miles per hour more – there had to be something saleable to aim for, a notable target to pursue. It led to cautious talk of the first 1000mph LSR, and ambitious minds set to the task of figuring out if such a feat was even possible.

Andy Green speaks to the press corps, having captured his first land speed record. Press Association

A look inside the desert pits ahead of the supersonic October run. Jeremy Davey, SSC

A Mach 1 banner is waved to signify the landmark supersonic run. Jeremy Davey, SSC

A triumphant Andy Green is held aloft after his heroics. Jeremy Davey, SSC

A jubilant ThrustSSC team tow the car back to the desert pits. Jeremy Davey, SSC

Craig Breedlove offers his congratulations to Andy Green, a wonderful display of mutual respect between two LSR legends. Jeremy Davey, SSC

Richard Noble celebrates ThrustSSC's return to the UK in style. Press Association

The record-breaking car was widely celebrated across the UK, and was met with great excitement when paraded through the streets of London. Press Association

Andy Green sits in the real Bloodhound in 2016. It's due to make a first public run in late 2017, but is it capable of 1000mph? Press Association

BLOODHOUND SSC
(and the future of the land speed record)

And so for now, that is where the story ends. It's been 20 years since Andy Green's historic supersonic run at Black Rock, and in the time since there have been no genuine threats to his remarkable feat – the longest time in the history of the land speed record it has stood unbroken.

That's not to say there haven't been contenders, or rumoured contenders at the very least. Ambitious teams began plotting, almost immediately, about how they might topple ThrustSSC, Green and Richard Noble; and they weren't looking to beat the champion by some small margin, as 1000mph became the target on everyone's minds.

After his 1997 triumph, and just like in 1983, Noble turned his attention away from record-breaking. But the lure of going fast had always proved too great, and when he got wind of a project he

thought might actually be capable of taking on the challenge he once again enlisted the services of Ron Ayres to help mount a defence. It was at that time, in 2006, that Bloodhound SSC was born.

To this day it remains the most credible and most likely car in production to lift the record, and with a theoretical speed of 1050mph it would be capable of making that certain piece of history also. There had been whispers that Bloodhound would maybe be ready in 2016, then possibly in 2017, but at the time of writing it has yet to make a public run – although at least one was expected before the end of the year. Early signs suggest that Bloodhound could be capable of achieving what it's been designed for, but there are serious obstacles to overcome.

The first is venue, because there aren't many places on Earth suitable for record-breaking that are long

enough to allow the acceleration, timed mile and then deceleration required for vehicles travelling at such speeds. Bloodhound's team believe the answer has been found in the form of a 12-mile track at Hakskeen Pan in South Africa, but the margins for error are small.

There is also the driver to consider. Green is a supreme talent, a trained fighter pilot, but the reactions needed to steer at the velocity being posited are close to what is possible for a human being. And what of his safety? He will have no ejector seat or shut-off – if something goes wrong the consequences would surely be fatal.

Then of course there is the vehicle itself, and while Noble's credentials speak for themselves even he and his team might not be able to find a way to prevent his creation from taking off as it blasts relentlessly across the course powered by a combination of jet engine and rocket power.

Given the incredible challenge they face, if Noble and Green can achieve greatness once again (and it remains a big 'if') it may well represent the final chapter in the thrilling tale that is the land speed record. It's sad to think that the great pursuit of speed might just have reached its limit, but Bloodhound SSC roaring to 1000mph and beyond would certainly be a most fitting end.

Pictured in 2011, this full-scale mock version of Bloodhound shows what the team is aiming for with its final creation. Press Association

Richard Noble poses with a model of Bloodhound SSC at an event to announce the project's launch in 2008. Press Association